Nedd Brockmann isn't afraid to d

running fifty marathons in fifty d

year-old had an idea: a 4000-kilometre run across Australia, averaging 100 kilometres per day with the aim of completing it in the fastest known time of 43 days. He wasn't chasing fame or public recognition. He just wanted to test his limits and raise a million dollars for homelessness in the process.

Most said he was crazy, others claimed it couldn't be done. But those who know Nedd knew never to doubt him. They understood that this is someone who will do whatever it takes to finish what he started, and that when he commits his mind to something, he always gets it done.

Understanding the mindset of someone predisposed to such feats of voluntary suffering has been nearly impossible – until now. With his trademark humour and unfiltered style, Nedd recalls the lessons learned on sporting fields that cultivated discipline, the setbacks that tested his resolve, and the relationships that proved most important of all: those who instilled the importance of hard work, of never giving up, and to always give back generously.

Praise for *Showing Up*

'Nedd is an absolute legend with a heart of gold. His run was spectacular and all the money he raised for the homeless was incredible. What a champion.'

Jimmy Barnes

'Among the many athletes pushing the outer envelope of human possibility, Nedd Brockmann stands alone – a young man who exudes a unique enthusiasm for life and rare authenticity that have made him a hero to millions of people across the world. In *Showing Up*, Nedd shares life lessons learned from his attempt to become the fastest man to traverse Australia on foot. Relatable with a dash of self-effacing humour sure to connect with a new generation, this book is a must read for anyone looking to extend their limitations and touch greatness in all aspects of life.'

Rich Roll, bestselling author of *Finding Ultra*

'When I chose to become a mother I believed it was my job to nurture these little people to become resilient, contributing and empathetic members of society. I think this book is my report card.'

Kylie Brockmann, Nedd's mum

'To double down on the present when there is only pain takes a Neddy-calibre heart. Unique lessons from a young man's perspective.'

Tom Hunt, close friend of Neddy

'If you need to feel inspired and motivated, to step out of your comfort zone and see what you are truly made of, this is the book for you. Nedd is one of a kind. If only we could bottle his heart, humour, grit and determination and take a daily dose.'

Carrie Bickmore, Australian television presenter

NEDD BROCKMANN

SHOWING UP

NEDD BROCKMANN

SHOWING UP

GET COMFORTABLE BEING UNCOMFORTABLE

SIMON &
SCHUSTER

London · New York · Sydney · Toronto · New Delhi

SHOWING UP: GET COMFORTABLE BEING UNCOMFORTABLE
First published in Australia in 2023 by
Simon & Schuster (Australia) Pty Limited
Suite 19A, Level 1, Building C, 450 Miller Street, Cammeray, NSW 2062

10 9 8 7 6 5 4 3 2 1

Sydney New York London Toronto New Delhi
Visit our website at www.simonandschuster.com.au

A catalogue record for this book is available from the National Library of Australia

ISBN: 9781761422133

Cover design: George Saad
Cover images: Bradley Farley
Typeset by Midland Typesetters, Australia
Printed and bound in Australia by Griffin Press

The paper this book is printed on is certified against the Forest Stewardship Council® Standards. Griffin Press holds chain of custody certification SCS-COC-001185. FSC® promotes environmentally responsible, socially beneficial and economically viable management of the world's forests.

CONTENTS

FOREWORD

I first came across Nedd like I'm sure a lot of people reading this book did. A mate forwarded his story to me with words to the effect of 'have you seen this', 'this guy is nuts', 'holy shit', and with several emojis with wide eyes and heads exploding. I'm not a runner and I don't think a lot of people swept up in following Nedd's journey were. But I am a lover of seeing humans push themselves because it reminds me that is where all the good stuff in life is, no matter what pursuit you choose, in the uncomfortable bits. Before he'd set off, Nedd's incredible choice of distance (one width of Australia) and audaciously inefficient choice of transport (one set of human feet) awoke something in us mortals. It was the feeling of 'he can't do this can he?', that gradually got replaced with 'holy shit I think he can'.

We were swept up, in real time, with watching an extraordinary example of what many of us feel the world needs more examples of – words that are easy to speak calcifying into actions that are much harder to do. Step by step, Nedd was doing it. People were chatting about it at the supermarket and in the pub. It spread in that wildfire way that people who sit in marketing brainstorming sessions hope for but money can never buy. The thought that sheer persistence could be an antidote for something that seemed impossible was intoxicating to us all. As we fumbled for our phones in the dark each morning to see what his update was, I'm sure I wasn't the only one who slunk off shamefaced after seeing Nedd had already run a half marathon and that suddenly my heroic efforts of getting kids ready for school didn't seem that impossible. His Instagram was hands down my favourite show of 2022 on any platform.

It was through my, let's be honest, fanboying his posts that we connected. (I may be wrong on this but I do honestly believe I may have come up with the hashtag '#Neddgendary' however sadly that isn't addressed in this book, probably cos it's too hot a topic so I'll save it for my own memoirs.) We chatted often during the run, and finally met up for real at the North Bondi SLSC on the night he returned. I got to meet his awesome mum and dad and Nedd shared stories from the road as I stared in slight disbelief at him hoofing into the not-world-renowned-athlete-recovery food of mini spring rolls. I've been very proud to be able to call him a mate ever since.

Not too long ago, I found myself in Queenstown, New Zealand, for a few days with Nedd where, through a bit of calendar acrobatics, we'd managed to wedge in a tiny boys' trip with another mate. Nedd hadn't been to Queenstown before and as the self-appointed tour guide I mentioned the local ski mountain Coronet Peak is a good mission to bike ride up. An unrelenting incline of about 8 per cent for about 8 kilometres, it takes a regular human amateur cyclist like me 45–50 minutes of grinding to ride it and it feels like an achievement every time. I mentioned it to Nedd that I'd ridden it, more as a fun fact (sounds cool going on boys' trips with me doesn't it?) and without a moment's hesitation his response was, 'I'll run it'. I've been up that mountain a bunch of times over the years and each time you see the odd cyclist and mountain biker, but I've never seen anyone running the road, even in summer, and this was the first week of the ski season. I was about to explain this to Nedd, but then I saw the slightly deranged glint in his eyes and realised I'd briefly forgotten who I was talking to. 'OK,' I responded, 'but look, let's go up before sunrise to beat any traffic. It'll be cold, there'll be snow for the last few hundred metres of elevation so I would say rug up. We'll obviously be at different paces, with me having an unfair bike advantage, so I'll summit then spin round and come ride your last few kilometres with you. Sound like a plan?' Nedd thumbs upped me. I tried not to let him see me begin to surreptitiously do calf stretches.

Cut to the next morning predawn, and a fired up Nedd Brockmann stands at the bottom of the alpine road shaking out his legs and rubbing his hands together. Dressed in shorts and a t-shirt, I assess him wearing my thermal bike gear and rain jacket. He must see the almost parental look of concern in my eyes and whips out a beanie to reassure me the cold has no chance. 'I should be sweet mate,' he grins. 'Let's GO!' Again, I'd briefly forgotten who I was speaking to. In the months since his run, he has become Nedd my mate, and whilst I'm of course aware of his feats and how I first heard of him, a lot more has fleshed out since then other than just a smiling ball of grit capable of running ludicrous distances. Coffees, dinners, him being the first to offer a hand or encouragement for something, I had got used to seeing Nedd in regular mode. That morning I was seeing flashes of him in battle mode. He had an objective in front of him and while he was cheerful and joking around, it was fading and he was becoming tunnel visioned. I smiled and we fist bumped and took off. Well, more accurately, Nedd took off like a dog finally allowed to run at the park, and I fiddled with my bike computer, like a dad who has too much gear. When I got underway ten seconds later, I was enjoying in a kind of weird way, watching Nedd run up ahead for a while while I reeled him in. Again, I hadn't forgotten he had this ability, but it occurred to me I hadn't actually seen it in the flesh apart from one particularly historic day in Bondi. While I watched him dig in up the hill my mind turned to settling into a rhythm that is essential for a climb like that, and pondered the maths of how much a guy on a bike would finish ahead of a guy on foot and what I'd say as I rode past Nedd on the upcoming bend. I was thinking a sincere 'you've got this mate' was supportive enough, without sounding too smug like I was rubbing it in that I was on a bike. While I was thinking these thoughts and doing the maths, I noticed a funny thing happening to the distance diminishing between Nedd and myself – it wasn't.

That trademark mullet, peeking out from under a beanie, illuminated by the splash of my bike light, was 50 metres ahead and inching further away. My breathing was heavy and my legs were beginning to burn as I found the pace I knew from experience I would need to sit on for the next 50 minutes in order to make it to the top. Uh oh, I thought, in a last ditch effort to protect my ego from having made a giant claim that was unfurling into a lie, he's gone out too hard. He's too excited. He's going to blow up. How embarrassing for him. But as the pain in my legs increased, so did the gap. A smile slowly spread across my face as I realised it hadn't occurred to me that he would beat someone on a bike up the mountain. I'd gone and done his favourite thing: I'd doubted him. Not because I had too much faith in my abilities (although no doubt I always do) or too little in his, just through my obviously now-wrong assumption based on physics that bikes are faster than humans. My 'you've got this mate' would not be needed. I watched the flashing safety light of Nedd continue to disappear until it wasn't there anymore when I rounded the corners. I only saw glimpses of it from then on, way up the mountain in the dawn light, attached to a running silhouette that looked right at home in that improbable setting of snowy alps. By the time I made it to the car park at the top of the mountain, he'd been up there for five minutes, still in shorts and t-shirt, standing in the snow beaming, steaming, and cheering me in. I rode past two guys on the mountain in full ski gear manning the entrance to the car park, staring at Nedd having just seen him run up and still trying to process it. One uttered to the other with a perfect Kiwi-accent, 'where the fuck did he come from bro?' And I swear I didn't add the 'bro'! It was a stunning moment. A micro reminder of what Nedd had done to us all in 2022. A smiling guy with a mullet in footy shorts having clearly run from somewhere he logically shouldn't have.

It was in the grind up that mountain where I was watching Nedd on the road up and above me that I realised what endurance feats were. They are not just about strength. They're strength multiplied by time. There is no endurance without time, and the sheer volume of not just the kilometres but the time Nedd was out there, enduring whatever was thrown at him, and that he kept doing it for a really, really long time, was the bit that elevates the feat. It's impressive to see a tree in the forest, but we're more impressed when we find out it's a thousand years old (well, not if you're my kids, but you know what I mean). That it has endured everything the elements has thrown at it and it refuses to yield. That's the bit that bends our minds. And I think if you'll allow me to finish easily the worst analogy in the book, that's what drew us all to Nedd – every day checking Instagram trying to wrap our heads around how much he had withstood and continued to somehow withstand. Like a mighty oak tree, running across Australia on little root legs, his leafy mullet bouncing out behind him. (Wow, that is powerful writing!)

During that time, we saw perhaps one of the greatest examples of what it truly means to make a decision. Not merely just have a hope, or a goal, or a want. A real decision. The Latin root of decision comes from two words that mean 'cut' and 'off', literally to cut off any alternative (well well well, look who's finishing on some research). For those 46 days across the country, Nedd showed what cutting off any other alternative truly looked like. A mindset that simply could not give up because it was never an option. But where exactly did that mindset come from? It was something we all wondered at the time and now I hope, like me, you enjoy tracing its origins in the pages of this book.

Hamish Blake

PROLOGUE: TRY AND BURY ME

Whatever happens, I will finish what I started.
There will be no easy way out.
Nedd

DAY 5. COOLGARDIE, WESTERN AUSTRALIA

By now, I am used to the night sweats. And the pain that must be treated. First come the creams: a smear of Voltaren gel, then Hirudoid to calm the inflammation in joints that threaten to burst through the skin. Then comes the cling-wrap to encase my legs. By the end of it, I look like a preserved specimen you'd find in a museum, prostrate and unmoving.

This is the time for recovery, a brief respite in which my bloodied and blistered feet are finally spared the bearing of any weight. This is the time for my mind to shut off, for the mental arithmetic of distances logged and calories consumed to cease, leaving me with empty dreams that do little to stir the imagination. Instead, all I can do is lie awake in a pool of my own sweat, staring at the ceiling of some decrepit road-house, running down the clock with each exhale that brings with it a wave of agony, questioning *what the actual fuck* I've gotten myself into. When you're pleading for sleep to envelop you quickly, it tends to desert you entirely.

But I'm used to it now. Or so I'm telling myself. Some 500 kilometres are behind me. I've been powered by little more than an hour's shut-eye each night – barely enough time to lower the heart rate, let alone rejuvenate the body. A surge of adrenaline stirs me in the morning before the drone of an alarm. We all know it will run out – it's just a matter of time. Eventually, I'll be steamrolled by sleeplessness, reduced to a shuffling corpse unable to summon the energy to run or keep my eyes open, any stumbles threatening to drop me under the wheels of a passing road train. I stare at the desolate stretch of road ahead – black-topped highway as far as the eye can see.

Sure enough, this morning my tank of adrenaline has run dry. I know it before anyone else. It's a tiredness that penetrates muscle and bone, a grim misery that weighs heavy on the chest, one that comes over those who know what it is to feel empty before the day's journey has even begun.

Some days, you get lucky. Pupils wide, scanning the darkness and converting any shadow into an identifiable object, while the eerie quiet acts like a shot of caffeine. Exhaustion falls away with each stiff-legged shuffle, such that the leaden feeling you started out with is shaken loose like an ill-fitting sock.

And then there are days when your legs feel lifeless. Days where the hurt and fatigue and the aching and stabs of pain accumulate, building atop one another, until there is no part of your body that doesn't scream when pressed. As I swing a leg off the bed and onto the floor, I know instantly: today, it's the latter. Better strap in for a dogfight.

MUM KNOCKS ON THE door at 3:50 am holding a bowl of oats. Concern creases her forehead upon seeing me, but she's quick to hide it. Smiling despite her weariness, she offers only words of encouragement as she reminds me of the job I have to do.

Even so, fear leaks out of the paper-thin walls of that room at the Coolgardie Oasis Caravan Park. My physio, Belly, massages muscles that seem to be locked in perpetual cramp. Feet are bandaged and strapped, hip flexors released, all in silence bar the groan of the coffee machine. My partner, Jemma, hastily packs away our gear, handing dirty clothes to Mum for washing at the next rest stop. Their eyes dart from each other to my own crumpled torso. Expressions shift from pity to panic to grief. An almost imperceptible shake of the head from Mum, and collectively they bite their tongue, knowing it's this they signed up for.

Each passing minute instils greater dread of the task ahead. I ease swollen feet into running shoes, whose soles betray the hard, uneven bitumen of outback roads. With the help of Jemma and Belly, I crawl into the teardrop trailer affixed to our ute. A doona and pillow, illuminated by a brake light, never looked so inviting.

I hear the engine roar to life, but I'm asleep before we've even left the carpark. Despite the single sheet of timber separating me and this makeshift bed from the road, and the lack of suspension that has the trailer bumping thunderously behind the ute's wheels, this is the one place where sleep descends. A delicious emptiness pulses through my body like blood behind a bruise, willing mind and muscle to shut down. I have neither the means nor desire to resist it.

Let it all be a dream. Let the thirty kilometres to the next starting point stretch on for an eternity. Let me sleep off this pain that burns like a fire within. Let the clock slow, so that I might sleep for longer, so that my body might adjust to this brutality. Let it not be 4:30 am.

Oh fuck. This isn't a dream.

I muffle a scream and Belly's face appears through tears. With the doors of the trailer open, he nods a firm yet supportive command to battle: 'Righto, mate.'

The clock is ticking. There are only so many hours in a day to get 100 kilometres done. Any time wasted now will steal hours from the night. It's time to get out the door. Time to get it done.

Alone now, my body ambles along the fog line. It wakes slowly, my features pulled taut as I struggle to push off with each footfall.

It is pre-dawn, yet there's little peace to be found on these roads. Jemma flashes her lights to alert me to a road train behind us, but I knew already it was there. The ground trembles and my breath catches as the monstrosity lurches ahead, shifting me off the road and out of rhythm.

Six days ago, they struck me as the stuff of nightmares: wheels big enough to swallow a man whole, exhaust fumes spitting dirt and debris the size of golf balls. The sleep deprivation, the muscular pain, the daunting kilometres ahead – all this I expected. But the road trains have been a new and unfamiliar enemy. Now, though, the thought of one clipping me doesn't seem so terrible. At least then I'd be out of my misery. What an easy escape! Instead, I subject myself to the daily grind: 100 kilometres per day, day after day; a battle waged against body and mind that consumes every waking moment.

There's no time nor spare energy to yell obscenities at these behemoths of the road. Every five minutes I duck away from their towering shadows, and every five minutes I'm reminded of their ferocity: roadkill splayed out on bitumen, the rotten stench causing bile to rise up in my throat.

It's getting harder to stay on schedule. Two-and-a-half hours to get twenty kilometres done. A thirty-minute break to get down mum's bacon-and-egg rolls, some coffee and whatever else my stomach can tolerate. Then I go again, and again, and again. Eyes on the clock, colour draining from the day.

The cold doesn't help. It claws at my layers, rattling my ribcage that strains with each intake of breath. There will be no warming up into this run. I've lost all feeling in my hands, with fingers so swollen and numb I can barely make a fist. As unrelenting headwinds batter me and belting rain seems to bruise any patch of exposed skin, I wonder what happened to the temperate climate western Australia is known for. These elements – and the 700 metres of elevation entailed in today's run (across what I was told is 'flat country') – all feel like a cruel joke. In some moments, the wind is so strong I can feel myself losing ground. The effort and exertion are there, but a glance at the GPS suggests it's all for little.

Metres accumulate to make up a single kilometre. The 12 hours 44 minutes that elapse to reach 101.23 kilometres seems like a month.

A SPRAY-PAINTED PINK LINE on bitumen marks the completion of another day's efforts. Shivering yet sweat-soaked, I lean my body into those of my team, a kind of protective hug we've come to practise for these fleeting moments of celebration. There's a collective exhale, an awareness that, against all odds, progress has been made. I want to savour it, to enjoy the satisfaction a little longer. But waddling to the passenger seat of the ute, I feel my body seizing up. Like coming to after a collision, it's pure survival mode from here, with knees battered and hips so tight that my whole body turns inwards with each step.

Jem reaches down to untie my laces. With careful and considered attention, she takes to shoe removal like a neurosurgeon approaching the operating table. A sudden jerk, she knows, will send a tendon into shock; a rough tug and skin will come loose with the sock. I gaze down at my feet, these two appendages I could once bear the sight of in thongs. Now, it would be a crime to display them in daylight. Toes swollen and wrinkled, they would scare children. Lack of aeration mixed with traces of truckers' toilet floors infuses them with a ferocious pong that stings the nostrils. If they look bad now, imagine what a further 3500 kilometres will do.

It hits me then. I have just seven hours. Seven hours to shower, get food down and complete the nightly mummification of creams and cling-wrap. Seven hours to shut down my body, so it might fire up once more come daybreak and be ready to knock off the next allotment of kays.

But how can you train yourself to approach things that way, when the future feels perpetually out of reach? You can't. The team knows this, too. Someone hands me a chocolate milk, and by the time the engine roars to life, my tongue is already desperately searching the bottle for dregs. There's the flick of an indicator, a brief pause, and then the crank of the volume knob as Creedence Clearwater Revival blasts over the stereo. Tunes that are familiar and beloved, tunes to get the mind off the task ahead. With my head pressed against the window, the icy glass numbs my forehead.

We drive the twenty kilometres to the nearest town, all for the promise of a hot shower. The team's spirits are high as we all scream lyrics, not caring about pitch or tone, just in a state of collective euphoria. I gaze out at tomorrow's route; the gradual incline, the slanted road, the desolate landscape that offers no buffer between the wind and me. Even with the team trailing me every step of the way, I know tomorrow's run will be yet another lonely dance.

When we reach the abandoned mining town of Widgiemooltha –'Widgie' to the locals – Mum and Dad have already done their homework. They've spent the last hour sorting out sleeping arrangements, scoping out a place to shower off the red dirt and salt stains I now wear like a second skin, and checking out the local bistro in the hope of finding an alternative to chicken parmi on the menu. It's hard to believe this place was once a populated township in the 1800s. Now, there's little to suggest occupancy. Miners stroll through the doors of the roadhouse, unloading their life on a barstool against a soundtrack of chickens clucking out back. But the town stands as a relic to a lamented past – a time when society coveted more than just the shiny and new, things that can be neatly packaged and presented on social media.

Just five days ago I felt the cool breath of ocean air at Cottesloe Beach. Now, the wind carries dust particles so large it's like sandpaper rubbing against your cheek. Each town is unique, but there's consistency to be found in the laidback charm that is the outback. The roads out here are hostile, the environment brutal. And yet for all the suffering, how can you not look up – and outwards – and see the beauty?

The moment of reverie vanishes as panic rises in my chest, threatening to manifest as a full-body shake. I lock eyes with Mum, who rushes towards the ute with a hand extended towards my door. I hold her gaze, the fear crawling across my face, and she stops. I ride out the shakes alone: first, an unbearable emptiness, then anger, and again that paralysing fear of the unknown that gripped me this morning. When it finally stops, I reach for the door handle and gingerly ease my body to the ground, one swollen leg after the other. Mum embraces me then and I can no longer hold it in. I'm twenty-three years old and crying with the ferocity of a newborn. The tears come thick and fast, and all I can do is grip Mum tighter, crying not from the pain I feel now, but in the knowledge of what's to come, knowing all the while that quitting is not an option. That stubbornness is something I'll never be able to shake, which means my future is predetermined, defined by sacrifice and pain.

ALL I WANTED WAS hot water at the end of a day's efforts. All I wanted was to feel the thaw of numbed fingers and toes and see steam cloud the mirror, so I wouldn't have to stare back at this reflection I can no longer recognise. But in Widgie, warm water isn't a given. Some days, apparently, it doesn't materialise, and you're left standing in a dimly lit bathroom, too tired to lift your shirt above your head, too tired even to weep as the water turns a biting cold, sinking you further into those murky depths of misery that you were trying so hard to avoid.

The quick rinse sends my core temperature plunging, or so it seems, and all I can do is shiver as Belly tries to calm me down. As I lie face-down on his table, he massages my legs. The pub is so close, but I doubt my ability to stand let alone walk. To onlookers, it must seem like the height of laziness: a man being driven the fifty-odd metres to the pub entrance. But everything now is about preserving energy.

Journey over, Belly opens the door of the ute, and he and Jemma support the weight of my body as I waddle inside to the table that Dad and my mate Bradley have reserved for dinner.

It's a weeknight, but every seat is occupied and it feels like the gaze of every local and transient miner is fixed on me. I don't blame them. At this point I'm a walking car crash, and everyone's just slowing down to check out the wreckage. I can feel my whole body screaming as I take my seat. Meal orders are placed and, as the smells of gravy and chicken salt waft through the swinging kitchen doors, my phone lights up like a pinball machine as messages from friends and strangers alike flood my inbox. I can feel myself coming apart. Slowly at first, then all at once. Ragged sobs seem to split my chest open and, as I look at my team, I feel a sense of distance wedge itself between us. I don't have the vocabulary to explain those waves of agony that wash over me now constantly. It's not something I can share, or something I can help them understand.

'I can't tell you how fucked up this is,' I splutter. 'It's so fucking hard. *So fucking hard.*'

Mum's chair slides back. 'I'm just getting service, honey,' she says, waving a phone in the air as she hurries out of the room.

The tears continue until I no longer have the energy to produce them and all that's left are salt crystals in my eyelashes.

Bradley looks at my battered body and invokes the wisdom of Hunter S. Thompson, who wrote about the ever-elusive 'edge'.

'You're past it, Nedd. You're in new territory now,' he says.

I can only nod, wanting to downplay the anguish I'm feeling. Had I the means to articulate it, my team would surely pull the pin on this entire operation.

Mum comes back, her face splotchy and red, betraying the tears she hid from my view. I wonder what she wants to say to me now but feels she can't. I wonder what verbal comforts she would offer to try to ease my suffering, but knows I would only dismiss. I wonder how hard it is for her to watch me unravel, to lose a piece of myself at each roadhouse at the end of another day's hell. I wonder how she sleeps at night, hearing my screams as I sweat through sheets and cling-wrap, only to appear at my door at 3:50 the next morning, bowl of oats in hand, smile fixed, words of affirmation at the ready. She knows me better than anyone. The people around me are those I trust with my life. But out here I'm a stranger to them all. On the road, eyes wide with the feral and ferocious spirit of the hunted, I crave only discomfort. I can't be sure of how dark it will get over the next few weeks, but I'm certain of one thing: whatever happens, I will finish what I started. There will be no easy way out.

WHEN I SET OUT to run the 3953 kilometres from Cottesloe to Sydney's Bondi Beach, the possibility of fame or public recognition was never a motivation. What I wanted was to test myself, to defy those self-limiting perceptions we all have of ourselves while also raising money and awareness to tackle the crisis of homelessness in our mixed-up society. I'd learned that Germany's Achim Heukemes had done such a run in 2005, setting a record of 43 days, 13 hours and eight minutes. I wasn't a follower or student of his running prowess; I simply felt that if he could do it, then surely I could, too. So, I set myself the goal of completing the distance in 43 days and 12 hours. I also wanted to raise one million dollars for homelessness, and when I heard from Noah Yang, founder and CEO of homelessness charity We Are Mobilise, I couldn't think of a better organisation to partner with. Noah and his team of volunteers focus on providing functional care and assistance to those in need. Their mission is to reconnect humanity and create change through connection, something I immediately felt drawn to.

We all have an internal voice, one that tends either to talk up our capabilities or play them down. Mine? Mine demands a mindset of: *Why can't I?* If someone else has managed to cross Australia on foot, running a hundred-odd kilometres every day over forty-three days, why shouldn't I be capable of doing the same – or going faster?

Since completing the run on 17 October 2022, I've fielded questions from people from all walks of life: athletes, business leaders, average Joes and Janes. They ask stuff like, 'How many pairs of shoes did you burn through over the course of the run?' Or, 'How are your feet holding up?' – posed, perhaps, with the hope of gaining access to an exclusive library of toe shots from my cross-country endeavour (God forbid anyone sees the video of maggots crawling out of one of my toenails).

Many want to know my diet secrets, as if my choice of milk was the difference between grinding out another 100-kilometre run and hitting the snooze button. Sadly, it wasn't. For the most part, though, people ask about the *how*. *How* did you keep going, even in those moments when your body felt like it might break in two? *How* did you cut through the noise, drown out the pain and negativity, and ensure that the one voice that kept telling you to push onwards was never snuffed out?

I've watched footage of myself answering those questions in public, and I've seen my eyes glaze over as I've offered my responses that were no more than a shrug of the shoulders. I know that if it's hard for me to articulate the depths of despair I found myself in out on the Nullarbor, then it's easier for others to dismiss my run as the actions of a crazed individual with a penchant for agony. 'Classic, Nedd,' some would say.

On the other hand, there are those who demand my body be subject to rigorous scientific investigation, as if there is some way to biohack your muscular system so it can withstand the most intense pain. Theirs is a tone of derision, suggesting I must be some freak of nature, comprised of a unique chemistry equalling unexplainable talent when it comes to pain tolerance. Whatever the explanation, what people don't know or forget is that I was taking on the unthinkable long before this particular deed caught people's attention.

A social-media following might allow you to inspire others and use your platform to champion a cause, but it won't see you forge on with only your demons as company, with shins swollen and a kneecap the size of your thigh. What people overlook is that I'm not a runner or an athlete of any kind.

I never ran cross country at high school or made the state athletics teams, and when it came to my athletic potential, often I was passed over for boys who were bigger, fitter and faster.

What most people don't realise is that I'm just a bloke who's built a life on the principle of showing up, every day. Testing my limits and pushing myself is a ritual, something I hold sacred. These tests of willpower lift me up in the morning and force me to become present. They are tests that make me a better person.

My guess is that you bought this book to learn more about my cross-country run, about the mindset that got me through it despite those periods when I looked cooked. But that mindset was forged long before the run. It was shaped in my adolescence, on the family farm in Forbes in the Central West region of New South Wales, where I watched my mum and dad rise before daybreak to get on with the job at hand without fuss or the need for attention. It was moulded at school, in classrooms and on sporting fields where I faced challenges – kids who were smarter than me, opponents who were more skilled, injuries that threatened to derail my ambitions – and stared them down. It was a mindset honed on lonely runs under the cover of darkness, where the sense of achievement was mine to experience alone. And it's a mindset that's been strengthened by encounters with powerful individuals and relationships that have helped make me the man I am today.

In *Showing Up*, I want to share with you the stories that have shaped my mindset most profoundly. These are the stories I told myself on those long and monotonous roads, where the wind stole the scream from my lips before I could make a sound. They're stories that speak to our potential, that urge us to push through our self-imposed limitations. They're stories that suggest we're all capable of greatness, as long as we're willing to put in the work.

PART ONE: A KID FROM BEDGERABONG

Don't come to me complaining or crying,
unless you're broken or bleeding.
Nedd's mum

1

My Mum, Kylie, swore she would never marry a farmer. But when she met Ian Brockmann, it seems the universe was determined to change her mind. Both grew up in Forbes, but farming was all that Dad had ever known. Despite helping his father daily with the labour-intensive tasks required on their cattle-and-sheep farm, he was never paid a wage. When he met Mum, his weekends entailed extra shearing work for any local farmers who needed sheep shorn. This was his source of income. The more sheep you sheared, the more money you made. And Dad was a workhorse: to this day, set him a task and he'll do anything to get it done. He worked 50-60 hours a week for his own father, then went out shearing all weekend. His whole life, he's never skipped a day's work. Maybe there's something to be said for his ticker, or for something else in the Brockmann bloodline that I was fortunate enough to inherit. Whatever it is, Dad is nothing if not dependable – someone you can rely on, loyal to a fault, never one to complain. Together, he and Mum make up the ultimate package.

Until we sit our parents down and find out what their lives were like before we came on the scene, we tend to forget that they are, after all, human. Just like the rest of us, our parents are prone to making mistakes, to giving their all and, sometimes, still falling short. But even in the periods when my parents were winging it, when they hid the struggles of farm life from their kids who grew up oblivious to financial uncertainty and years of drought, I have only ever seen them as superhuman. And with time and acquired knowledge, that superhuman strength that each projects has, to my mind, only grown stronger. They are the best teachers I've ever had.

I can't know everything about the time they spent together before I was born, but here's what I do know: the greatest feat of endurance I'm aware of occurred between the years of 1996 and 1999, in the absence of camera crews or a social media following. She may not have garnered headlines but what Mum went through needs telling.

In the New Year of 1998, my maternal grandmother retired to her bed and essentially never left it until she passed away just under a year later. She'd been diagnosed with breast cancer eight years earlier and, ever the stoic woman who downplayed any misfortune or discomfort, what she described that night as a sore neck would later be revealed as the return of cancer, only this time it had metastasised into nearly every bone in her body. Doctors would tell her that the cancer had progressed to such an extent that had she sneezed around that time, she would have broken her neck. She was flown to Sydney, where an ambulance took her to hospital for a three-month stay. Given this was a time preceding the ubiquity of mobile phones, it marked the first time Mum hadn't spoken to her own mum every day. The two of them were best friends and confidantes. They shared everything. And when Mum experienced a stillbirth between my older brother Logan and me on 4 August 1997, losing the son she would name Benjamin, it was her mother who helped her through the months of grief. It was also her mother whom she first informed of her pregnancy with me, when my grandmother finally returned from the hospital and settled into her bed.

Mum had never inquired, mid-pregnancy, about the sex of her first two babies, but after suffering the stillbirth, she required frequent scans and blood tests and wanted to know the sex of her new baby as soon as possible so that she could begin developing a relationship with him or her. Dr Somes, a GP who had treated my grandmother and was now treating Mum through her pregnancy (and would later become our family GP), told her she would be having a boy. My mum told her mum she would call the baby Nedd. It was something for just the two of them – a secret born of love and trust. Together, they had conversations with and about me, speaking to Mum's growing bump with a special tenderness, soothing those stirrings that rippled beneath the flesh.

I would have given anything to have been able to meet my grandmother, this woman who was so pivotal to the shaping of my own mum. But I never got the chance. Three weeks before I was born, she died on 17 December 1998, leaving Mum without her best friend and biggest supporter. To have experienced two great losses in such a short space of time is cruel, and yet the day my mum gave birth to me, there was no cloud of sadness hanging over the delivery room. She wore my grandmother's wedding band and, as if sensing her presence, infused the room with a mood that was much like the cocoon of warmth the pair had created together in those months leading up to my birth: calm, tranquil, tender. With Dr Somes presiding over the whole thing, the birth went smoothly. Mum was induced and, within half an hour, went into labour.

At one point, a nurse said to Mum, 'That's such a beautiful wedding band', to which Mum responded, 'It was my Mum's.' Knowing what Mum had been through, those in the room expected a flood of emotion, for the arrival of new life to be overshadowed by the memory of a passing. But Mum could only look at them with kindness and serenity, assuring all that it was fine. With the ring on her finger, she felt a closeness that transcended space and time. My birth was peaceful, easy, as if overseen by some greater force.

Twenty-four years later, Dr Somes retired. In his three-decade career, he supported patients through moments of unimaginable sadness and the kind of joy that makes the heart swell. In thirty-one years, he delivered thousands of babies and watched some couples leave the hospital with no baby at all, carrying the kind of personal tragedy that stays with a family forever. He saw Mum through three pregnancies and one devastating stillbirth, as well as the passing of her own mother. Upon retiring, he asked Mum a question.

'You know what I tell people was the highlight of my medical career?'

'You're going to tell me Nedd's birth,' Mum said.

Dr Somes nodded. 'Yeah, I am.'

He then confirmed the mystical presence Mum felt in the delivery room on 11 January 1999. He spoke of the ease of labour, the incredible peace that seemed to settle over the room like a fine mist, and the exceptional strength of the woman at the heart of it all.

2

The Brockmann farm is situated sixty kilometres west of Forbes in the quiet town of Bedgerabong. I always think I'm home once I reach Forbes with its friendly inhabitants, but then I remember I've got another half-hour drive before I'm on the driveway that feels instantly familiar. As soon as I feel the crunch of gravel under foot or wheel, I sense the years dropping from my shoulders like an oversized coat, drawing me back to my childhood and the freedom it entailed.

Bedgerabong Public School lies halfway between Forbes and home, with skinny, tar-paved roads crisscrossing the land that sits either side, green and vast and populated with cows and sheep. Floods have rendered the roads barely drivable, like some kind of Mario Kart racecourse, pot-holed and bunged up so it's only the local driver who can be confident of navigating them without serious mishap. Houses become sparser as you drive west, until eventually you have to squint against the horizon to make out any house at all on properties that stretch for as far as the eye can see.

With the Lachlan River serving as a guide, the road continues for another seven kilometres, until a big bend sees you land on a sixteen-kilometre straight that you follow all the way home. You count the farms that go past: one, two, three . . . each offering sightings of cattle, hay bales, irrigation and fencing. Two little bumps appear in the road, sending you momentarily airborne as you strike them at a speed close to 100 kilometres per hour. That's when you know you're home. And sure enough, the sign 'Brockmann Trading' looms large, before your eye lands on the mailbox, one that's survived now for two decades since Logan and I first welded it together. Modelled on our own farmhouse, it features a piece of aluminium tin that covers a little box like a roof. It's skew-whiff now, but Mum and Dad have never wanted to replace it.

Entering the farm, you can see the shed, filled with machinery or hay, and some kind of seed that Dad has sown peeking up at you from the ground. The colossal marks of tractor tyres seem perpetually imprinted in the earth, while Dad's older cows – now in their twilight years – can be seen grazing in the front paddock, with more of them visible in the distance as a cluster of white, black and brown. Even having spent my childhood and adolescence here, I can never quite comprehend the sheer scale of it all. Thousands of acres, blanketing the landscape, and even then, stretching further still into a never-ending backdrop of dusty tracks and forest trees.

To think this was our playground as kids, that we could spend hours every day exploring it without ever nudging its boundaries. It was here I came to appreciate the feeling of finding myself forever and ever alone out here, with my own thoughts as company. With nothing to compare it to, I consider my childhood relatively normal. It's only when

I relocated to Sydney at the age of 20 that I came to see the gift my siblings and I had received by way of independence from such a young age as something novel and profound. We were free! Within limits, we could do as we pleased. As long as we went to school and made it home, we could have the filthiest haircuts, swim in the dam, go yabby catching. We were never bored.

Mum had two ironclad rules: never come to her complaining or crying unless we were broken or bleeding, and always be home before dark. She didn't much mind where we were or what we did on the farm, so long as we were back in her sight with a trace of light still left in the day. And she sensed that we would be, back at the sliding glass door in time for dinner, if not for the company then for the insatiable hunger that seems to stalk you through childhood and adolescence. I don't know if Logan and my younger sister, Mabel, were quite as adherent to these rules as I was, but to me they were cardinal.

Aged eleven, I got a motorbike. It was a birthday present, something of a tradition in our family so we could help Dad out by using the bikes to round up sheep and cattle into the yards. I was pushing it along and trying to kick it into gear, but I was too small for this bike, and to get on it, I had to run alongside it and, with pinpoint timing, jump up when I'd achieved the necessary momentum. I was only 200 metres or so from the house one morning, when the front tyre hit a heap of wire on the ground. The bike collapsed sideways, throwing me off and into a mound of khaki weed. After the shock dissipated, I glanced at my dirt-stained elbows and the deep scratches I'd taken to my torso and bare legs. Rising, I stared at the bike – defeated by a roll of wire – and kicked it.

'Piece of shit,' I muttered.

Nothing was broken, at least. Nor was there any deep cut oozing blood. So, I marched to the tool shed, grabbed a pair of pliers that I held high as I returned to the scene, and unleashed my fury on the wire that was now caught up in the bike's tyres.

When finally I'd freed the bike, I struggled with the weight of it, summoning every ounce of strength contained in my eleven-year-old body to lift it. Eventually, I got it going again, and drove off towards the creek.

Hours later, I returned home to find Mum standing in the kitchen. She called out to me before I'd even come in the door.

'How are you going, darl? What's happening?'

I shrugged my shoulders. 'Nothing much. Just went for a ride.'

Mum met my gaze. 'How was the fall?'

I had no idea she'd watched the whole scene unfold from the kitchen window. She'd seen my body crumple under the bike, and she'd waited for my cries to get louder as I approached the door. She'd waited for me to tap on the glass and plead for the kind of care only a parent can give.

But the tears never came. Instead, Mum watched as I found a solution to the mess I'd gotten myself into, and resisted her own urge to go out and help. She let me believe I had all the answers, that I was capable of more than I thought. And with a bit of thought and effort, I'd managed the little calamity on my own. To my mind, I was just obeying the family rule: don't go off complaining or crying unless I was broken or bleeding. And as long as I had my mum to look up to, I'd honour those words.

Dad would love nothing more than for Logan and I to work on the farm alongside him, but he's never put that expectation on our shoulders. Rather, Mum and Dad wanted only for all three of their children to grow up into happy, healthy, functioning adults who would contribute to society more than we ever felt the need to take from it. They wanted us to reach our potential in whatever it was we chose to pursue. They never forced us to be something, nor did they try to mould us so that we'd fit into a particular box. They watched as other parents pandered to their kids, pressured them to follow a particular career path and otherwise tick the boxes that somehow constitute success in modern society. My parents set an example of responsible non-conformism. And they let each of us evolve into our own person.

Mum wanted us to be resilient, to think for ourselves and problem-solve. Though by presence alone she was a disciplinarian, Mum's every action was grounded in absolute love. She'd told me of the times she sat exasperated at the kitchen table, trying to spoon-feed me at fourteen months old. Rather than oblige her, I covered my mouth with my hand, refusing her attempts at feeding until she eventually slammed the spoon down on the tray of my highchair. She turned her back to me, trying to conceal her frustration, and when she finally regained her composure and turned back around, ready to give it another go, she saw me sitting there, spoon in hand, feeding myself expertly. I wanted her care and attention, yes. But from a very young age, I also wanted to do things on my own.

And that's the thing about Mum. Though she nurtured us into the people we are today, she also knew when to let go. Our days on the farm were coloured with the enthusiasm that comes with unchecked curiosity and endless exploration – and without the self-consciousness that comes when you know your every action is under the watchful glare of a parent. Logan and I would head out after breakfast, with Logan serving as the ringmaster. He'd concoct every sort of wild and brazen plan. Mabel often knew better than to fall into line, but I was never able to refuse Logan or reject his idea of a good time. So, when he said, 'Nedd, this is a really great idea: hop on the back of this pushbike – I'm going to tie a rope to the motorbike and fly you around really fast,' all I could do was hop on the bike and hope for the best.

3

Bedgerabong is a small, neighbourly country town with only one primary school for all the kids in the vicinity. At Bedgerabong Public School back in my time there, there were twenty-six of us in total, making up the grades of pre-school through to Year 6. Once, at a school working bee, my friend Ollie dared me to jump from the platform to the fireman's pole while we were standing around in the playground – a distance beyond my six-year-old capabilities. I missed the pole completely and fell awkwardly on my arm.

Immediately, Ollie called out to the parents.

'Nedd's hurt himself,' he yelled, his eyes wide in disbelief as he appraised my disfigured limb.

By some stroke of luck, one of the parents helping out that day was a radiographer who worked in Forbes, and she sat in the front seat while Mum got me into the family Nissan Patrol and buckled my seatbelt. Together, they put two rulers on either side of my arm, stabilised it with sticky tape and had me place it on the armrest.

The road to Forbes was covered in potholes and all manner of debris, and each bump knocked my arm out of place and sent a wave of pain through my body. Mum kept glancing at my reflection in the rear-view mirror. When she turned around to ask how I was, all I'd say was, 'I'm good', as a single tear rolled down my cheek. The look on her face was one of disbelief: why wasn't I blubbering with a broken arm? After all, *that* would have been acceptable. Broken or bleeding? Check. I could have complained and cried as much as I wanted to. But I didn't. I wouldn't have been able to explain it then, but my mind was already focused on feeding my body positive messages.

Years later, the feats of endurance I sought out and undertook would make sense to Mum. They would help explain all those moments when, while raising me, she questioned why I wasn't acting like a normal kid. At the time, she couldn't grasp exactly what it was. She'd think, *Well, that's just how Nedd does it . . . but is this normal.* There was no parenting manual in her bedside drawer, no parent she could turn to who'd gone through something similar with their own kid. The question that plagued her most was, *How do I parent this child – because I can see something happening here that I've not experienced before?*

To all of her kids, she gave something more than any book could provide. She gave us her time. She gave us her undivided attention. Every trip into town or school might include a substantial, uninterrupted conversation with a mother who wanted, above all, to build a relationship with her kids that could withstand anything.

SCHOOL WAS HARDLY JUST around the corner from our place. To get there, we'd drive thirteen kilometres to the bus stop, where we'd be the second group of kids to board, staying for the 45-kilometre drive with either Russell or Wendy – the bus drivers. All up, door to door, it took us ninety minutes to get to school. For extracurricular activities, however, on weeknights and weekends, it was Mum covering that entire distance in the Patrol. Monday would be reserved for saxophone lessons or drama, and we'd train for soccer on Tuesdays, attend swim practice on Wednesday and rugby training on Thursday nights. Friday would be the Forbes swim club and Saturday the rugby match, followed by soccer on Sundays.

Each week after swimming time trials at the club, we'd be treated to dinner at McDonald's, where we'd order chicken nuggets and Happy Meals. When the paper bag emblazoned with the big 'M' logo was presented to us, Mum would order us to 'check your nuggets'. For a while, I didn't understand what she was on about, brushing it off as one of her strange, yet endearing, quirks. But there came a time on one of those long drives home when one of us would cry out, yet again, 'Mum! I've only got four nuggets in mine!', that I began to see she was only being smart.

You'd think few things could be worse than being cooped up in a car with your mum for sixty kilometres, but on those trips, we solidified bonds that went beyond maternal responsibility. You can't choose your family, but I would choose mine again and again because ours is a closeness born not purely of proximity but of deep connection.

Mum and Dad wanted all three of their kids to have the opportunity to find themselves and become adults away from home. They wanted us to be responsible, generous people and felt such qualities were best instilled from a young age, away from the over-protective gaze of a parent.

Consequently, when it came time for Logan to start high school, they decided to send him to Kinross Wolaroi School in Orange as a boarder. And as soon as they met with the principal, it was decided: Mabel and I would follow suit – each of us would start boarding school in Year 7.

But even when we were boarders, we still communicated daily. It was thanks to our connection that we would talk to Mum on the phone and she would be able to tell instantly just from our tone of voice – or those things we *didn't* say – if something was wrong or if we were struggling with something that maybe wasn't even yet obvious to ourselves.

4

Perhaps my parents' most powerful lesson of all was that we are what we do, not what we talk about or say we'll do. My Dad is a man of action. For as long as I can remember he's led by example, never voicing a negative thought or complaint, but always showing up and getting on with the job at hand, day in and day out.

If, for my siblings and I, there was a sense of freedom in being allowed to explore the farm, for Dad it was different: he *had* to be out there, and he was usually alone. When you've got more than 1000 cattle to maintain, time is a precious resource. Before daylight had even peeped in through the blinds, he'd be awake, toiling away outside so as to give us kids the kind of opportunities that he'd never had growing up.

From 2010 to 2014, I watched Dad display his signature commitment to routine when the land surrounding our farmhouse had turned impossibly dry and dusty. The lush green that had once seemed so permanent had all but vanished, leaving in its stead patches of brown and beige that extended the length of those giant paddocks. Without the cushioning of grass or vegetation, the ground felt like rock, and was suddenly dangerous to kids zipping around on motorbikes with no regard for safety.

As the months turned to years, neighbouring farmers gave up and sold their livestock, but Dad never lost hope. Day after day, he kept showing up, modelling both calmness and a quiet conviction that things would turn around, that it would rain soon enough, and all would be right with the world.

At the time, I had no perception of just how hard those years were for Mum and Dad, of the stress that arrives on the back of drought, compounding with each year that brings inadequate rainfall. It wasn't that we kids weren't curious; Dad simply never let on. He shouldered the burden alone, instinctively protecting his family from the inevitable struggles of the farming life. He would walk in every day after hours of dusty toil and, with his tone light and jovial, say, 'Hey kids, how's it going?' Then he'd listen to our stories about the day's adventures or what so-and-so did at school, and still he would not speak of his own hardships because Dad saw those as all part of his job. Just like how Mum reinforced to all of us that we weren't to complain unless we were broken or bleeding, Dad never complained about the work he had to do.

What a role model Dad is. He left school just shy of his fifteenth birthday. Farming is all he's ever known. As soon as we could walk, we'd be outside helping him with various tasks. He'd have us in the tractor, our hands on the steering wheel and his feet commanding the brake and accelerator as he taught us how to drive it so we could do it on our own one day. But there was never any pressure to commit to a life on the farm if that wasn't what we wanted.

For those four years of drought, Dad showed us all how to get through something. There is usually pride involved in not giving in, but his actions were never borne of an inflated ego or a desire to be seen. Simply, they were the actions of a father looking to provide for his family. In doing just that, he taught us that you never quit.

Nowadays, I can see Mum and Dad's influence in all of us. We may have taken different paths, but those daily lessons instilled on the farm are still evident in the way we comport ourselves, in the people we choose to have around us, in the way we interact with others, in the integrity with which we live our lives.

I see the effect of our upbringing in Logan, a gentle, caring empath who is a great father to his own kids. I feel it in his hugs, in the way he doesn't just put an arm around you but sweeps you up in both, making you feel untouchably safe. Just like Dad, he's reliable, someone who is capable and gets on with what needs doing, always with his kids in mind.

And Mabel, the little dynamo, one of the most caring and compassionate people I've ever known. She radiates warmth in any room she enters, as well as a charisma that's infectious and draws others to her like moths to a flame. For all her kindness, she's also driven and doesn't hesitate to speak out on the things she believes in.

All of us are products of our parents, of these teachers who have, all being well, guided us with love and unwavering strength throughout our lives. More important to them than any tangible success, any accolade or achievement, is that their children are good, caring people, that we strive to give back more than we take in this life. And when you have that kind of relationship with your parents and siblings, when you're encouraged to become your own person, how could you want for anything more?

5

At Bedgerabong School, our afternoons were spent playing sport. Weekends saw Mum drive us into town for competition, and while we did everything from swimming to athletics to soccer, it was rugby that meant the most to me.

When I was ten, the sport moved from the light graze of touch footy to the aggressive shock of tackles, causing me to edge closer and closer to the sidelines. Seeing a defender come running at you, his eyes ablaze, can be enough to make you stop and hand over the ball, apologising for any inconvenience caused by those few metres you stole while in possession.

I wasn't fearful of anything growing up on the farm, but on the rugby pitch I felt timid, almost frightened at the thought of being tackled and hurled flat on the ground as players trampled over me in pursuit of victory.

In one match, the whistle blew for half-time and before I could make my way off the field, Mum ran up to me.

'Nedd, I am not bringing you to these football games if you are scared to tackle someone,' she said, holding my gaze. 'Get out on that field and use your shoulder – you know how to do it.'

Ten minutes later, I ran back onto the field and looked at Mum standing there on the sideline alongside the other parents, most of whom hadn't had to drive for an hour to the game. I didn't want people to think I was scared, especially Mum. After all, the woman had a point. All I had to do was keep my head low, like the coach had shown us in training, and use my shoulder. It's like the coach told us: *You're more likely to get hurt if you're timid and hesitate in a tackle, than if you follow through with conviction.*

It was time to start playing properly. Time to compete. As soon as I made my first tackle, I felt a rush of adrenaline that propelled me to make a second. The change in my attitude was astonishing and parents turned to Mum to ask what she'd said to me earlier, wondering if she could knock some sense into their sons.

With Mum watching on, I felt invincible. Along with a handful of other kids in my year, I came to excel at sport, entering every event in the swimming and athletics carnivals and coming away with multiple medals. If things continue this way, I thought, surely I'd be headed to the Olympics as the next great Australian heptathlete.

And so, I couldn't wait to follow Logan to Kinross, knowing that as a boarder I'd be able to expand my sporting prowess.

PART TWO: MORE THAN A RUNNER

I've found a sense of power in that – to have sat with discomfort and stared down defeat, to have given both the middle finger.

Nedd

6

My eyes scan the aisles of the Woolworths in Orange, though I don't know exactly what I'm looking for. Confectionery seems too juvenile, as do those biscuits whose advertising targets young children via cartoon bears with big eyes and cheeky smiles. I watch Logan practically raid the shelves, ever the consummate professional when it comes to identifying those food items that sustain you through the school term when the meals provided to Kinross boarders come up short on flavour and quantity.

'Nedd, you've got to get Gatorade,' he yells from down the aisle, holding up a large tub of the powdered drink that grabs your attention like a neon sign, all oranges and sickly hues of green.

I nod enthusiastically, taking the tub from him and dropping it into my near-empty basket. Then I follow him as he strides towards the noodles section.

I only ever wanted Maggi noodles, that comforting cup of warmth that followed afternoons of sports practice and long drives back to the farm. But the start of high school demands a show of adult sophistication. Now is not the time to give into our childish wants. It's time to grow up. Logan puts enough tubs of Mi Goreng into his trolley to feed an entire year group – and I promptly follow suit. Satisfied with our choices, we walk back to the counter, where Mum waits patiently, knowing the day has come to send her second son off to boarding school.

The drive from home to Kinross takes two hours, and each kilometre seems to intensify the excitement churning deep within my belly. I crane my neck out the window as Mum turns into the long driveway marking the school entrance, and I gaze up at this structure that looms like something out of the Middle Ages. Manicured lawns flank grand buildings, the grass cut into neat checkers of varying shades of green. There's not a misplaced leaf to be found in garden beds that belong in a *Better Homes and Gardens* catalogue – all dazzling florals and neatly pruned shrubbery. Looking at the main oval, I can't shake the feeling that the entire student body of Bedgerabong School would not fill its bleachers.

Walking past the original school building, Wolaroi House, I see a campus boasting a heritage that came long before I arrived and will continue long after I leave. I look down at my shoes, polished and shined to such an extent that I can almost make out my own reflection. Back home, Logan and I roamed the farm like a rat pack, wearing bruises from our adventures like badges of honour, our hair wild and free. Now, I find myself kitted out in a blazer and tie, no mullet in sight. I can barely recognise the young man I'm being shaped to become.

Older kids walk through the school in groups of three to five. Those in Year 12 are already sporting tufts of facial hair. Their bodies stand erect. They have the hard-earned posture that comes with gym-room diligence: broad shoulders pushed back and down, biceps pressuring the sleeves of their school shirts. Intimidated, I don't dare look any of them in the eye. Compared to these young men, I feel like a kid playing dress-up; everything fits too loosely; everything hangs baggy off my tiny frame.

Aside from Logan, who's three years ahead of me, I don't know anyone here – I have not a single friend I can beeline towards in the common areas. In the Year 7 boarding house (known as Trathen House) I see a seat free on the long couch and grab it.

'Hey, I'm Nedd,' I say, introducing myself to the kid next to me.

He nods slowly in acknowledgement, before finally looking up. 'I'm Pete,' he says, offering a lazy wave of his hand.

'You shoot guns?'

'Yeah,' says Pete – '.22-250.'

'Nice. Me too.'

Turns out there are a lot of country boys here, boys who grew up on farms just like me, shooting targets before they were old enough to memorise their five-times tables.

Pete also has an older brother in Logan's year. With this level of connection, it's safe to say we've become friends.

Like most of the other new kids, I've turned up with a phone, but we're promptly told to put these away. The boarding master tells us that students' use of phones will be confined to an allotted hour. Whether we choose to use that time to call home is up to us.

There are four of us to a dorm room, each with two bunk-beds and a small cupboard for each boy.

In my room, we're all too excited to sleep, talking long after the lights have gone out and the boarding master has yelled at us to be quiet. There's Joe, a swimmer who already seems to possess the gym-honed physique of a late teen; Harry, whose ballet training sees him glide across a room with a quiet energy; and Cheese, a country boy who grew up close to Bedgerabong and is a motorbike fanatic. I can't know at this stage whether they will become my best friends at school, or whether our bond will be simply one of proximity, but having come from such a small town where there weren't even enough kids in my year group to fill a table, I'm grateful for this opportunity to make friends and, maybe, find out a bit more about who I am.

7

I take my sky-high confidence in my athletic abilities from primary school to Kinross and get a rude shock. When I hit the water at the swimming carnival, I suddenly realise that I'm not the prodigy I thought I was. Rather, I've exited the small pond that was Bedgerabong. At Kinross, I'm lining up next to kids who are twice my size; guys carrying the kind of muscle that must be partly the result of regularly scoffing protein powder. At Kinross, my days of sporting excellence have abruptly ended.

Being born in January, I'd started school a year younger than most of my year group. What that means in the pool is that although my limbs are flailing frantically in the 50-metre freestyle, often hitting the lane ropes, and although at the finish I'm pulling myself out of the water gasping for air, I'm nonetheless being advanced to the next competitive stage because of my birthdate. Technically, I'm still meant to be competing against Year 6 kids. So, Kinross selects me to compete with the best from schools in the local region in my age division.

With my fellow reps across each year group, I'll be boarding a bus at 3:30 pm this coming Friday that will take us to the carnival in Bathurst. Everyone seems to be looking forward to the trip and the thrill of competing. Not me, though. I've made a decision: I'm not going. No way.

On the phone to Mum, I tell her I'd like to come home for the weekend. She agrees to come pick me up.

When Friday afternoon arrives, I see those kids I'm meant to be travelling with boarding the bus. With just one seat still vacant, a teacher stands at the bus door, studying a clipboard with the roll attached. I know it's me they're waiting for, but I can't bring myself to go over and explain myself. What would I say? That I'm not going because of fear? Fear of failure? Because that's it. I don't think I'm good enough to compete against these other kids. And having compared myself to guys in my year group, my anxiety extends to my body, which I'm now self-conscious about. I'm so much smaller than average. Where others stand tall and imposing, I'm just this string bean of a kid whose muscles haven't caught up to his height.

I slip out of the school gates and find Mum's car, and all the tension drains out of my body. On the drive home, she can't believe my excitement at coming home for the weekend. She knows that the thrill of being in a new school and away from home had dulled any sense of homesickness, and it shocks her that a weekend on the farm is something I've been longing for. Sadly, my relief is short-lived. By the time we feel the crunch of gravel under our tyres as we swing into the driveway, Mum has received an email from the head of sport, alerting her to my absence and the delay it's caused the team, who apparently waited on the bus for me for fifteen minutes or more.

I want Mum to cover for me, to help think up some elaborate explanation for why I had to be picked up and driven home as a matter of urgency. Between the pair of us, we should be able to come up with something convincing, right?

But Mum doesn't want a bar of it. She sits me down at the kitchen table and tells me how the weekend will unfold. I'll write letters to all the teachers I've let down and accept full responsibility for my actions. And after she drives me back to school on Sunday night, I will spend all of Monday morning seeking them out individually so I can apologise in person. Even the thought of having to swim in front of hundreds of spectators is far less terrifying than this.

Come Monday, before first class, when kids are throwing a football between themselves, or catching up on the weekend, or completing an assignment that's due in a matter of minutes, I start making my round of apologies. I find the swim coach and, with my head lowered in shame, hand him my letter. He accepts it, and studies me with curiosity as I splutter, 'I'm really sorry, I'll never do it again. If I make the team, I assure you I'll come and I will compete.'

Perhaps sensing the turmoil that had cost me a weekend's sleep and the courage I've had to find to face this moment, he can only smile. 'That's all right, mate. Thanks for the apology.'

I nod, sincere in my regret, and go on my way, finding the rest of those I've let down until no more letters remain.

None of them look particularly cut up about the whole thing, nor do they make a fuss about my disappearance. But to Mum it is imperative that I accept responsibility for my actions and understand they have consequences, great or small. She knows that if I don't, I'll do stuff like this again. That I'll run away from something hard or challenging rather than confront it, not just as a schoolkid but for my whole life. Mum never pushed me down a certain career path, but she did want me to be a man of my word. And as I'm learning from her now, that means understanding that spoken commitments carry weight, and that to be seen as someone dependable and loyal means if you say you're going to be somewhere, you show up.

Rushing to my first class, I no longer feel a sense of shame or fear regarding my sporting abilities. I'd skipped out on the swimming carnival simply because I didn't think I could measure up to those around me, because I felt unworthy of competing against kids who were bigger and stronger than me. But I also remember just how much I loved the competitive scene at Bedgerabong: the carnivals, the nervousness before a race, milling about the canteen and sharing the medals around as everyone cheered for one another. I was so excited anytime we hopped in the backseat of the car, Logan in the front and Mabel next to me, heading into town just so we could kick a football around the park or swim laps in a pool that reeked of chlorine.

THE SCHOOL YEAR SLIDES by and, as December approaches, a lot of students who perhaps also felt there was something special about them as athletes begin dropping out of their respective sports. At Kinross, they've found themselves coming up against guys who are more skilled and talented, guys whose bodies just want to hold muscle. At Kinross, they find they're no longer the best at anything.

Me? I don't want to be left without hope and passion simply because I'm still a kid finding myself, growing up, exploring and nurturing new interests. I have heart and

I know that when I commit to something, I never do so by half measures. I'm all-in, always. Whether I grow over the summer break or not doesn't matter. I will outwork anyone, even the best and most gifted kids.

Thankfully, though, a new crop of swimmers emerges that means I'll never have to compete at a regional swimming carnival again.

8

Rowing suits those who love structure, who are driven to push themselves daily, who rise before the light of dawn has caressed the window, already dressed and headed for the gym or water, ready to give their all. But these traits and propensities aren't easy to cultivate in schoolkids.

Rowing also favours those with a lean but strong build, tall individuals with long arms (or levers). No matter how strong your mind is, no matter how committed you are, the fact is that physique is imperative. You can have the biggest heart, but still there'll be someone with longer arms, more strength, and the ability to pull harder than you ever could. Still, what you do when you come up against someone like that is up to you.

At the end of Year 7, I was still struggling to remember where some of my classes were on campus when I dressed in my sports gear and headed down for the rowing trials. In the gym, the coaches had set up various tests designed to identify the best candidates. You would have to meet a set of criteria to be considered for the team and any bench-warming positions.

Shifting my weight between each leg in a nervous dance, I watch as a kid in my year called Mungo steps up for bench-pulls – an exercise performed stomach-down on a weights bench set at an incline that roughly simulates the rowing action. By some miraculous confluence of genetics and appetite, Mungo already weighs 110 kilograms. Some say he's still growing, and that he had hairs on his balls at the age of six. Without a moment's hesitation, he lowers himself to the bench and picks up the weighted barbell in both hands. He then proceeds to pull it up to his chest at speed, his breath coming in sharp bursts as his rep count climbs. Mungo is making this look easy, as though he's been asked to tie his shoelaces.

When it's my turn to step up to the bench, I realise just how thoroughly Mungo has deceived us all: his sweat covers the bench. My arms shake merely from holding the bar, and as soon as I'm positioned to start pulling the weight towards my chest, my whole body goes rigid with the stress of a load that's too heavy for me. It feels like an hour goes by before I manage even one pull. I get one more out for a total of two before the coach dismisses my efforts with a wave, probably alarmed by the look of distress that's plastered on my face.

We make our way into the erg room for a one-kilometre time trial. The space is set up as four rows, each with five rowing machines, with another two up the back. Each of us chooses a machine and we adjust our foot straps as we wait for the coach to signal the start of the time trial.

As soon as it comes, piercing the air with its shrill tone, all you can hear is the punch of exhalation, and soon the air turns pungent with the scent of body odour that clings to our uniforms. I have never felt such devastation as upon hearing the smashing of a handle against the screen upon release, as someone completes their kilometre – and still you have another 300 metres to go.

My time is slow compared to the other boys', but I want to row so badly, even if it means not being in the top boat. I have watched Logan get into the sport, and now I want to share in the delight of winning races and standing atop podiums at regattas. But more than that, I love the discipline of the sport – the early starts, the constant need to show up ready to fire, to get on with the job. To this point, it is the most demanding physical pursuit I've chosen, but I refuse to back down.

ONE MORNING, I SOMEHOW sleep through my alarm. Waking up bleary, I stare at my watch on the bedside table in horror. I have only two minutes to make it to the bus that'll take us down to Spring Creek for the morning's rowing session. The bus leaves each morning at 5 on the dot. That's one thing about rowing: it teaches you punctuality. Show up late and you'll miss the session. No one is going to wait for you, no matter what sort of hotshot you might be out there on the water. I pull on my zootie and rush out to the bus bay, but it's too late. Three minutes past five. I can't even see the blink of a brake light down the road.

Sitting on the cold ground, I wedge my feet into my sneakers. I know the route to Spring Creek after following it on the bus three times a week – five kilometres on dark, winding roads – and I'm going to run it. It's dangerous – and certainly I'll cop a rebuke from a teacher or two should they find out about my little adventure – but I will not miss a session. I set off at a clip, my breath fanning out before me like a wall of fog.

The sun is just peeking up over the water, casting ribbons of pearlescent beauty across its surface. As I near the destination, I can just make out the shapes of my peers standing along the banks. Seeing me flying down the road, their expressions turn from confusion to shock. 'What the hell are you doing, Nedd?' a friend yells.

The session is already under way, and it annoys me that I let myself miss a moment of it. I scamper to the boat shed, grab a scull and matching oars, and hit the water, my heart thumping against my chest as my frozen fingers wrap painfully around the oars.

When I emerge from the water at the end of the session, the coach approaches wearing an expression of mock consternation.

'Nedd, you can't run outside of the school grounds. You just can't. It's not allowed.'

I nod, aware I've overstepped. Then I look him in the eyes, and instead of apologising or groping for an excuse, I present the doctrine I now live by: 'I can't miss a session. I'm sorry, but I can't *not* show up.'

The coach doesn't say anything else, then or later. Perhaps he knows what it's like to chase something wholeheartedly, to want something so much that it dictates your every action. Perhaps he knows what it's like to be constantly told 'no', that 'you're not good enough', that you're no match for bigger, stronger opponents.

Regardless, there was no way I was going to roll over and sleep in that morning. I was going to get to training, by whatever means.

THERE IS NO EASING into boarding school. In a flash, you're on your own, and rather than having your parents there as disciplinarians, you have the hierarchy of year groups – which can be painful.

In Year 8, all of us move into a fourteen-bed dorm room, located on the same floor as boarders from Year 9 through to Year 12. Our room is located right at the end of this long corridor, and roughly once a week as we head to our rooms after our final lesson of the day, we're met by more than twenty Year 11 and 12 boarders, all lined up on either side of the hallway.

'Tunnel of love, boys!' one yells, like a war cry. And in that moment, we know what's coming.

We drop our bags and brace ourselves for attack, legs split-stepping before we take off, quick as a flash, down the hall, our heads down and elbows driving back, gathering momentum with each stride.

Of course, no matter how quick we are, we never get out unscathed. The older boys step out, sending us flying with a swift tackle or shoulder charge. Kids come up a mess, their school shirts ripped and spotted with dots of red. Others are sandwiched into a corner and unable to speak for some time, too traumatised to recount the details of what should have been a simple return to their room. One kid even gets his arm broken. Despite its regularity, we never get used to the Tunnel of Love but rather live in fear of it, skulking in the shadows, flinching at any sudden movement as though a rampage might occur at any moment.

9

I spend the whole of Year 10 looking forward to rowing camp in the New Year. December arrives with its blue skies and unrelenting sun and we students leave the school in a stampede, clutching empty Tupperware and bags overflowing with dirty clothes. We spend the holidays at home, reunited with our families. And when the New Year comes, it's time to head back to an almost empty school. It's just a small group of us who shuffle into a boarding house with our sports bags and rowing kit, eager for strenuous days in which every hour will be filled with exertion.

Since my first taste of rowing, I'd longed for these mythical five days spent on Spring Creek, where a strict routine would surely create a powerful sense of purpose.

Between five in the morning and six in the evening, we complete three intensive training sessions. By nightfall, we're wrung out like rags, barely capable of making dinner-table conversation.

At rowing camp, every session is a test. We do seat racing, where you have to hop in a boat with three other rowers, and then they take one kid out and put another in during a nonstop series of 500-metre races. This goes on and on until we're spent, hunched over, arms dangling out of the boat, lactic acid swamping the body. Then the coaches do the calculations to find out who is the day's best rower.

Mount Canobolas looms large in the background. We're dropped at its base and told to make a running ascent as a team. Of course, the older boys go out hard and leave the rest of us behind, thinning out the cluster we'd started out as. Soon enough, pushing into the rarefied air, you feel alone up here. When everyone has finally made it to the top, the bus returns us to the campgrounds, where we collapse, aching muscles forbidding further movement.

Our performance at rowing camp determines who makes it into the top quad for the new school year. I leave camp hopeful, knowing I'd given my all every minute of every day, while others had taken chances to slack off whenever the coaches were distracted.

But each year I wait for the list to go up, and each year I'm disappointed. There is never a place for me.

In the same circumstances, other boys just quit. And they spend the next few months in a kind of trance – shocked that you could sleep in every morning until a few minutes before first classes, that you don't have to physically wreck yourself if you don't want to, that you can choose comfort over suffering.

Come Year 10, from 5 am, we do two hours of training on the water. Some days, we row for distance – between 13 and 15 kilometres. Other times there are interval sessions, where we row hard for seventeen strokes and easy for five over a two-kilometre stretch of water. When the session is over, we pull the boats back into the shed and take the bus back to school, where we shove whatever food we can find in the dining hall into our faces before running up to our rooms to change ahead of class.

Lessons pass in a blur, and just when it feels like the early start is catching up with us, draining us of all energy, the final bell rings and we're in the gym, obliged to complete a strength session followed by an hour on the erg, feet out and core engaged.

I can scarcely envision a day that doesn't involve some sort of physical hardship or test of endurance. So, I stay in the team, believing my chance will come.

Meanwhile, Mabel starts rowing and wins a bronze at Nationals, while Logan proves the best rower of all of us, collecting multiple medals at Nationals in the schoolboys coxed four and seat-racing for the New South Wales Under-19 men's eight. It hurts, watching them succeed with such apparent ease.

I keep my head down and plough on, working harder in the gym than anyone else, knowing someone could get injured or sick and then I'll get the call-up to sit in the quad. I believe in my own ability, even if no one else can see it, and I believe my time will come, that I'll get there eventually. But year after year, that hope is dashed with the posting of the top quad.

My whole school life, I never do make it into that boat I dreamed about. But in the summer before starting Year 12, it's announced at the rowing dinner that I will be rowing captain. At camp, as per usual, the bus drops us at the foot of Mount Canobolas, and the coaches tell us to run to the top as a team – from the scrawny thirteen-year-olds to the bulky-framed boys just shy of eighteen.

Once again, the cluster thins as the older boys sprint ahead, leaving the younger ones to navigate the rocky terrain alone. Finding myself among the frontrunners, I turn to look behind me. I see the stragglers slow to a crawl, or else stop completely and put their hands on their thighs.

I run back, hollering at them to keep going. Like a cattle dog, I herd them back into a group, encourage them to keep pushing, reassure them the end is in sight.

Briefly, we all become a single group again, but then, inevitably, the thinning process restarts, with a forlorn trickle of runners bringing up the rear.

Again, I turn and descend, play cattle dog again as best I can. When the final straggler and I reach the top, the boys who are in line for the first quad – the genetically gifted ones – are already on the bus, and they barely register our arrival let alone the toughness these young guys had shown. They're tired and just want to get back.

SINCE PRIMARY SCHOOL, I've only ever spoken my mind. Mum has always said to me, 'You're allowed to ask questions and seek answers. As long as you do so respectfully, I will support you.'

I see everyone as a person, not as their job title, and as a result, I sometimes challenge figures of authority when I see them acting unfairly. At school, it often seems to me, students are given special treatment or certain privileges because of family connections – a brother who was a sporting hero – or thanks to their own athletic prowess. I tend to speak up about it and call out the things I perceive as wrong, but that doesn't do me any favours with teachers or friends alike.

Me at about six months old with my dad. Note the birth mark on my forehead. Thankfully it disappeared over the next year.

On our farm with my beautiful mother Kylie holding my little sister Mabel and my older brother Logan.

Moments after the final whistle blew for the Forbes Platypi to win the 2017 first-grade Blowes Cup premiership. Pure elation! This image gives me goosebumps.

The final day of my fifty marathons in fifty days. Lloyd (left) and Pat (right) paced me to run a sub-three-hour marathon – the first time I had ever done so.

Everyone celebrating the end of my fifty marathons in fifty days. I couldn't believe how many people turned up!

My good mate Tommy and me after I finished running 200 laps of the Bronte hill car park loop. Cooked as a chook.

My beautiful girlfriend Jemma. We've been through some pretty epic times together over the last few years. I'm grateful to have her in my life.

Karl Stefanovic and myself on the *Today* show. I've never been more nervous in my life. Not because I'm in my Budgy Smugglers packing very little, but because I am telling half of Australia what I'm about to attempt.

The route we travelled across Australia.

Meet Bertha. Mum and Dad purchased Bertha and slept in her every night of the trip. This was our on-road kitchen and where many a deep conversation was had, usually between myself and Mum.

This is the teardrop trailer that I was supposed to sleep in. However, after the first three nights, I couldn't bear the thought of sleeping in it. We kept all my snacks in it when Bertha wasn't near.

This is the ute set-up that mostly Jemma would drive (occasionally Belly when Jem took a much-needed break), either in front or behind me while I was running.

Cottesloe Beach in Perth the day before the start of my run. Thanks to Case Construction, I think this was the first time there had been two front-end loaders holding up a start banner on Cottesloe Beach.

If school is where you're meant to find yourself, it's also the place where the demand for compromise feels strongest. Values are traded for popularity and those things we believe in are steamrolled by a yearning for acceptance. Often I feel like I'm trying to be someone I'm not, that I'm working overtime to come across as someone who doesn't have particularly strong convictions, who'll laugh at others and trade insults as though they roll off the tongue. But that isn't my character.

At the same time, I can't understand why those kids I see as friends don't show up for me in the same way I do for them, why their words don't carry the same weight and commitment as mine do.

Eventually, I stop trying to fit in, stop trying to be like everyone else. And by giving myself permission to be the person I want to be, I found the core group of friends I've always wanted. These aren't friendships built on happenstance. They're more solid than that. I'm drawn to these people by their way of seeing the world, their morals, and how they make me feel in their presence.

So, there's no denying the great lessons I'm learning at school. But these are still tough years for various reasons. As the excitement of starting boarding school fades and disappears, I feel homesick for life on the farm. My inability or refusal to be a sheep, to follow the pack, means I'm cast as a kind of outsider. Yes, I have close friends. But when everyone wants to be part of a big group, I find myself on the fringes, the conversation washing over me.

A lot of kids seem to think that school will define them, that the success or otherwise they find in these hallways will follow them through life. But I suspect popularity means nothing beyond campus – and nor does the ability to kick a football. Those things that are valued at school are nothing if you haven't had to work for them.

I feel good about my own learnings on life, for the mentality I've cultivated in the halls and on the fields of Kinross, because I know they'll serve me well for the rest of my life. And as I walk out of those school gates for the final time, I feel ready for the wider world. No matter what I choose to throw myself into, I know there'll be no one who'll outwork me. I mightn't have achieved amazing success here, but I've learned from the experience. I know there's a big world out there waiting for me, and I'm equipped to strike a blow.

10

My schooldays over, I become reflective. I think about who I am and the forces that are shaping me.

Ian Brockmann is a man of the land. Growing up with two sisters on a thousand-acre farm, Dad was expected to help out from a young age. He was never paid for those countless hours that were sliced from his adolescence, but the issue of compensation never made a difference to his work ethic. Each morning, he'd ascertain the job that needed to be done, pull his hat low over his brow and get to it. By the age of fifteen, school was little more than an inconvenience. There was too much to do, too many responsibilities that fell on his shoulders, to be much bothered with it. And by the year's end, he had all but stopped going as he had pig sales to attend. When he eventually took charge of his own farm, that same discipline only intensified.

Through my childhood, before the sun had appeared on the horizon, Dad was already out of the house, preparing the feed. He'd tend to perimeter fences that keep the cattle in, enduring the unrelenting heat, usually without company or assistance. On those days when I could help him with sheep or cattle work, I found myself confronted by a workhorse I didn't have the engine to match. There was always more to be done, something else that could be fixed or improved, and none of it would ever be put off until tomorrow. Outdoors, Dad ran out the clock, working until he had nothing left to give.

Crops were sown around May, when the air blew cold and the days were short. By late October, they were ready for harvest. Though Dad was always busy on the farm, come harvest time there was a frantic energy about him. Harvesting is a major operation with so many moving parts – the machinery required for harvesting grain; the tractor, the chaser bin to store the grain before it's emptied into a truck; silos that stand empty only to be full by day's end. The stakes were too high to leave anything to chance. One break in the chain and everything collapses. All of us had to help during those six weeks, sharing in the collective purpose. Just about all year, a farmer hopes for rain. But at harvest time, you crossed your fingers and hoped none came.

When I was ten, I drove the chaser bin that followed the header that edges along the length of the paddock. When the weather held and there was no dew in the cogs, we'd go all day. I'd get the signal and speed down in the tractor, emptying the grain into a truck that would then drive back to the farm, allowing us to repeat the process again and again until the paddock was done. Some days, we got lucky. A small paddock might take just four hours to complete. But for those paddocks that stretched on for two kilometres or more, we were out there for days.

I'd return home just as nightfall settled across the farm, thinking my job is done for the day. Mum would be busy in the kitchen as we set the table, our stomachs grumbling. There'd be little scope for conversation as we inhaled our food, but Dad's seat remained vacant. He'd stay out while we ate, caked in a film of dust that clung to his clothes and skin, rendering his face expressionless as he ensured the trucks were empty and the silos full, all so we'd be good to go again first thing in the morning.

When we finished dinner and started preparing for bed, there would be just the lone blink of the oven standing alert like a lighthouse, guiding Dad to his plate of steak and mash that sat behind the door, concealed beneath a sheet of aluminium foil that quivered from the slow and consistent blow of the fan.

Ian Brockmann is the hardest working person I know. If you were to venture out of Forbes and let yourself be guided by the Lachlan River to the big bend that sends you on a sixteen-kilometre straight to our family farm, your eyes will scan the horizon and see a solitary figure focused on some task. His clothes will be dust-covered, much like his shoes, which bear the scuffs that come with wear, but he will be grinning. He will be casting his eyes across the land he knows so intimately, and he will feel proud of all that he has achieved: this farm that is thriving under his care, a care born of an understanding that those things we want in life aren't given to us but must be earned. He won't grumble or complain (unless you're next to him in one of Mum's group fitness classes). He will not speak of his daily routine in the exalted manner of someone seeking recognition or praise. He will simply do the work, moving quietly and purposefully, in his eyes nothing but a keen appreciation for all he has.

I DON'T KNOW WHAT I want to do now I've left school for good. In my last weeks there, careers officers had visited and asked us to consider our futures. They'd talked about skills and employment opportunities, about the interests and passions we held outside the classroom. They'd talked to us about the subjects we enjoyed and excelled at, about the subjects that didn't come quite so easily, about test scores and expectations. They handed us a quiz that was supposed to match our strengths to our most suitable career. I remember ticking various boxes and rating various parts of my personality on a scale. Though the interface of the online test was new to me, it took all of a few minutes to complete. Even so, it acted like it knew me better than I knew myself. *An outgoing personality. A keen interest in adventure. You should be a pilot, Nedd.* I'm not buying it.

The conversations between kids would extend into recess and lunch. When we'd usually be running around a field, chasing some kind of ball, we'd instead sit about with inquisitive eyes, asking one another: 'What are you going to do after school? What are you going to be? Where do you want to go to university?'

Friends talked about careers they imagined for themselves. Some had clearly defined trajectories, as though nothing could possibly go wrong and everything was guaranteed. They saw the degree and the graduation, the car they were going to drive, the house they'd buy and the lifestyle they'd lead. There was no room for distraction, no time for a gap year or the licence to dabble in this and that.

Talk of the future buzzed around me like a swarm of flies, the words indecipherable. I had nothing to contribute to the chat. I didn't know what it was I wanted to do or who I wanted to be, or how anyone else would know for that matter. The idea that you should know what you want to do for the rest of your life at the age of seventeen felt crazy and dangerous. You're yet to see the world or have a decent range of experiences, yet to find yourself or know what it means to have a clear sense of identity, let alone form your own.

I saw in my peers anxiety around others' expectations. Before we'd even left school to enter the wider world, there was this sense of urgency to find a career path and see it through. Fortunately, Mum and Dad are putting no pressure on me to have all the answers and I want my friends to have the same grace. I want to tell them that they're allowed to take their time, that there's no rush, that they can try something and realise it's not for them and that won't make them failures. They see success as a straight line when I suspect it's more likely a snaking path. Chances are, I reckon, staying the course purely because you think you have to won't lead you anywhere good. Better to give something a shot, and if it doesn't fit or doesn't inspire you, then leave it behind and resume the search for your true passion. I understand it's a privilege to live for a purpose, but should an opportunity present itself, why not grab it?

I flirt with the idea of taking a gap year and travelling, but Mum has me reconsidering as soon as I bring it up.

'Oh yeah, and with whose money are you going to do that?'

She has a point. I don't exactly have the funds to be jet-setting around the world right now, no matter how much I might learn in the process.

But since the careers officers told us to consider our outside interests and hobbies, I know I need look no further than sport. I never made the first quad, but rowing has given me a self-discipline that I don't want to let slip.

Back home, Forbes Rugby Club is looking to put a strong first-grade team together for the 2017 season. The players have been talking and the consensus is that this will be the season in which we give the competition a shake. Rugby has been a love of mine ever since Mum first started shuffling us to and from town for training and matches. Of course, opponents are much bigger now than they were in primary school – some weigh as much as 120 kilograms. They run at you without fear and with destructive intent, and even if you're not trampled and manage to make the tackle, you get up dazed, maybe winded. And then you're back in the game. The best way to stop these big guys? As my maternal grandfather, Snow, always said, 'They can't run without legs, Nedd.'

One of the head coaches at Forbes calls me up, asks if I'd be interested in coming to training. The last time Forbes won a premiership was 2003, when my Uncle Dave (Mum's younger brother) was team captain and fullback. Since then, success has dried up, replaced by missed opportunities and losing streaks.

When I finish the call, I'm excited about the season ahead. Here is the chance to be part of something: a community of people wanting to play footy in the pursuit of winning a premiership. And if I choose to play rugby, I'll be able to spend more time with Dad on the farm. I think back to those days at home, waking early to find Dad outside, hours of work already under his belt. I think of how lonely it must be out there, miles from the house. Dad never held any expectation of us coming back to the farm after school or choosing that life for ourselves, and he watched as Logan chose to be a builder and went straight into an apprenticeship in Orange after Year 12. But I know that I can learn a lot from working with Dad.

I call Mum. 'I'm going to come back and work with Dad on the farm for a year. And I'm going to win the Blowes Cup premiership with Forbes.'

Mum doesn't skip a beat. 'Go for it,' she says.

11

I'd been getting ready for some smooth sailing. I thought I'd get home and it'd be like I never left, that I'd slip back into those days when I went out and helped Dad with the cattle or the sheep as soon as I was old enough to ride a motorbike. But I forgot that those 'days' weren't really days at all. They were a couple of hours' work.

Even on weekends when he'd needed an extra pair of hands, I'd be heading back to boarding school on the Sunday, anyway, never spending more than a day and a half out in the paddock. And for most of that time, Dad had trusted me to get my little job done while he went off to do his own tasks. Now, suddenly, we're in each other's faces constantly, and it's proving to be tough for both of us.

'Hooo! Auughhhh! Turnthefuckit!' come the cries. I turn to see Dad, his arms flailing above his head, screaming gibberish at me while gesturing towards the scene in front of him.

Out in the paddocks on his motorbike, Dad can just look at cattle and know where he wants them to go. This is his playground. The man can look at the lay of the land and know from what direction you need to come to herd these beasts. It's second nature to him, as easy as brushing your teeth. I thought I was handy on the farm. And I *am* really good with cattle and have a keen sense of anticipation, but that sense pales in comparison to Dad's. The man is quick. He acts instinctively, without pause or second-guessing. The fact is, I'm always two steps behind, and Dad doesn't know how to communicate what he's sensing. All this comes so naturally to him that nothing registers as thought. It's all just instantaneous action based on gut.

It's all I've heard now for two months: torrents of yelling that rarely contain fully formed words, except 'fuckwit', which seems to punctuate every second sentence. This was meant to be a year in which we'd grow closer, but it feels like we're drifting apart. We can't even communicate with each other. What does that say about our father–son bond? Unable to contain it any longer, I go on the attack.

'Dad, what the fuck are you saying?' I scream. 'Do you know that actually doesn't help anyone?'

But he's not about to concede anything, and when I kick the bike into gear and start heading back to the house, all I can hear over the rattle of dirt under the wheels is his yelling carried on the wind.

Inside the house, I don't wait for Mum to look up before launching my tirade.

'I can't do this. I can't help him if he can't fucking talk to me.'

Mum comes over to where I'm pacing the floor and motions for me to sit down.

'Nedd, you need to take a step back,' she says as I try to calm my breathing. 'It's not him, it's you.'

Confused, I search her eyes for clarity.

'You need to realise this bloke has never had to communicate with anyone,' Mum says. 'He does it to me, Nedd. It's not what he does, it's how you respond. If you continue to get upset about the way he's talking to you, I'm telling you now, I've been married to him for 30 years and he ain't changing.'

Understanding registers on my face and Mum nods in encouragement. 'It's how you respond,' she repeats.

When I head out for work the next day with Dad, I wait for it to happen again, knowing something will arise that I can't get a grasp of fast enough. Sure enough, the explosion comes, but I hear Mum's words in my head and rather than lose my cool, I take a moment to gather myself.

'Dad, can you please just sit down for two seconds and explain how it is you want this fence post straightened? Also, explain how you want these sheep pushed up. Explain how you want this paddock sown. Just explain. Please.'

He's quiet, seemingly realising for the first time in his life that the problem has been not so much the questionable intelligence of the person working alongside him as his inability to provide coherent instruction.

Encouraged, I press on.

'Tell me in the best detail you can and then I'll work out the rest. But if you're coming at me yelling, my immediate reaction is to bite back at you. I'm going to come back firing. Let's just talk it out.'

Let's just talk it out. The words become something of a mantra for us. And in their repetition, we find a shared appreciation for each other. The days pass and we come to a new understanding, one that hadn't been possible until now. I see just how hard he works, and I understand what

Mum means: this is what he's done all his life; it's all he's ever known.

I hadn't understood just how hard the work was until it became a fixture in my daily routine. With new manpower available to him, Dad puts me to work on the fifty kilometres of fencing that the cattle are now trampling over. It all needs to be knocked down and rebuilt.

The summer heat is remorseless: you step out of the house and into a furnace, your skin immediately prickling with sweat. So, I rise at four to get a head start on the day, knowing I'll need to be done by midday to avoid the worst of it. I take barbed wire and walk it out between strainer posts in one-kilometre lengths, dragging it all the way back before pulling it taut. Every four metres, I hammer in a steel picket with a motorised steel-post driver that weighs twenty kilograms. It takes three days to complete a one-kilometre section, and at the end of each day I return home with hands scratched and bleeding from wire digging into flesh.

It takes me the whole year to finish the fifty kilometres. Each morning I go out there, I think only about how Dad managed on his own for so long. Imagine it! Your sons and daughter are off at school, your wife is in town, and you need to do the fencing because your cattle are getting out.

During my stint, occasionally I have a mate help me with the work or someone else who comes to lend a hand. But even then, I can't escape the loneliness. I find myself looking forward to rugby and the people I will meet, breaking up my days of work on the farm with their familiar faces and friendly conversation. For so many years, Dad has done it all on his own. And for all that time, he never let on just how hard it is.

12

The first-grade coach comes up to me at the end of training. 'D'ya kick, son?' he asks.

During the trial games, it was impossible not to feel a sense of optimism about the coming season. Everyone wants to be in the first-grade team, to have a shot at winning a premiership. I've never kicked a goal in my life. But if it's going to help me get in the team, there's no doubt that I can learn to. Besides, surely the coach just needs to know that we have a back-up kicker on the field in case something happens to the main goal-kicker during a match?

'Yeah, fucking oath I kick,' I say.

'Great,' says the coach. 'We've got ourselves a goal-kicker.'

When the team is named for the first-round match and I'm selected in the position of fullback, we stand there like a line-up picked at random. Aside from the shared uniform, there's little that ties us together as a cohesive unit. Most of the boys are farmers from around town, others are welders – guys used to manual labour and hard effort. A few of the players I've heard of: back in school, they were elite, and some even went on to play first grade for some district or another. Gradually, however, new priorities have snuck up on them. This is a team of battlers: guys who love beers on the weekend, guys who rock up to training because they have to, not because they want to, guys whose sense of self-worth isn't wrapped up in footy. They have kids, real jobs and limited time. They know what it means to juggle responsibilities. But still, they don't want to give up the community and camaraderie inherent in team sport. And so here we are – the Forbes Platypi first-grade team, all of us believing that this will be the year we do it. This year, we will win.

Midway through the season, the Platypi are sitting within the top three teams on the table. On Tuesday and Thursday evenings, we huddle under the lights of Grinstead oval, our cheeks flushed and our breathing fast, except for Hally, our hooker, who thinks fitness training isn't important. Fresh out of school, I'm the youngest on the team by a couple of years at least, and I still inhabit the mindset I'd cultivated while rowing.

I'd arrived at 6 pm, thirty minutes before training starts, just to do my run-throughs and stretches before practising my goal-kicking. I've told no one that kicking is new to me. I simply absorb as much information as I can from watching YouTube videos on how to kick, trying to develop a technique and routine that I can improve each week.

By the time I've completed a thorough warm-up, the boys are just starting to get moving. Tracksuit pants are reluctantly removed as the guys start grabbing their ankles, pulling legs behind them in a quadriceps stretch. The enthusiast among them jumps up and down for a second or two before thinking better of it. Movement is kept to a minimum as conversation flows easily, all of us in on the joke as we take to ribbing one another.

'Jesus Christ,' says Brad, our inside centre and owner of the town's local pest control service. 'I wish my asshole was as tight as my hammies.' Laughter fills the air as we take to the field, ready to run through our plays against the boys in second grade.

Our captain, Jack, is a guy you'd love to have on your team but would hate to face as an opponent. He's forever in blokes' ears, picking battles for the sake of it, using dirty tactics in the ruck, all while being assertive and as tough as hell when the moment requires it. Tonight, though, he hangs back, talking on the sideline with the coach and general manager. His absence follows us around the field like a shadow, the usual barking of orders replaced by silence.

I wait for someone to step up and take charge, but no one does. We look to our best player, Mahe, our halfback, but he's shy and softly spoken, more comfortable simply doing his thing than instructing others on their role.

'Oi, Jeffrey, come round! Sharpie! Come, come!' I yell out. 'Roll, roll, roll.'

Minus conscious thought, I start providing direction. And my voice doesn't break but instead rings out loud with unshakeable confidence. From the sidelines, Jack watches this youngster rising to the occasion, filling the breach, unafraid to boss around this group of older guys in their twenties and thirties, who together have years of experience as a team. And the boys listen to me. There's no eye-rolling or ignoring of the kid, just a tacit respect evident in their trusting eyes as they follow my commands.

It's a respect I've earned in games, from making the right calls in attack, making astute defensive reads. Jack is our captain, but no one player makes a team. As we stagger off the field after training, there's a building momentum. It's palpable here and it's palpable in the change rooms at halftime. Winning the premiership is no mere pipedream. It's something we all think is within our reach.

13

By lunchtime, Grinstead is already packed with visitors from neighbouring towns, all of them here to watch our knockout semi-final against the Bathurst Bulldogs. Our clash will be the last of the day, and each passing hour sees the crowd swell, so that by kick-off at 3:15 pm, every spare inch of grass is occupied.

I'm filled with a nervous energy that I see reflected in the eyes of my teammates. The stakes are high now. Whoever wins this match will proceed to the grand final, where they'll take on the Orange Emus, the team that has become universally hated (outside of Orange) for the ease at which they win seemingly everything. It's a winning streak that's proven impossible to end. The tournament is theirs to lose. But our team isn't one to believe in stories of favourites and underdogs. We just play our hearts out.

Ten minutes into the game, disaster strikes. My right knee is driven into the ground under the full weight of my own body and that of a prop whose knee lands on the back of mine. Through all the grunting and heavy breathing, I hear and feel a pop. You know it's bad when your knee goes hot from the inside out. When my opponent climbs off me, I stagger to my feet and look at to my kneecap, sure I've done damage. Uncertainty overwhelms me and seems to dim the pain so that all I can feel is a numbness as my thoughts turn to problem-solving. I take a step and stumble awkwardly as the referee awards our team a penalty within kicking distance.

I've kicked for goal every game this season, gradually becoming more reliable and earning the faith of Jack and the rest of my teammates. Regardless of the pressure, I can get the job done. Every game, I've approached the tee with confidence. But now it feels as if the ground on which I stand is unstable. I line up the shot from a friendly angle, knowing this should be easy. I've done it enough times now that the action is second nature to me. Fully fit, I could land this shot with my eyes closed. But this time I spray the ball well wide of the posts. I'm hobbled: I just can't get my right leg to function. As I rejoin my teammates and register their sunken expressions, I can only think, *What the fuck are we going to do?*

The clock is winding down and only two points separate the teams. We lead Bathurst, 20–18. It's a battlefield. Stud marks cover the ground, shirts are mud-stained and torn, and players bear the cuts and grazes that come with hard knocks and rough ground. We keep trying to seize the momentum and run away with the game, but our collective energy is low. In fact, everyone is spent. All either team can do is try to outlast their opponent.

With six minutes left, a pass to our winger near Bathurst's try line is intercepted. The guy is going to chip and chase, I can feel it, and as I see him sprinting towards me, I know I'm the last line of defence. If he makes it past me, he'll score.

If I don't tackle this guy late, it's a certain five points for the try. If I tackle him late, I'll be penalised for a professional foul, but there's a chance the Bulldogs will miss the three-point penalty shot.

I tackle him late.

The whistle blows as we tumble to the ground. Wincing, I get up and see the yellow card the referee has thrust into my face. Hobbling off the field, I see the horrified look on my teammates' faces: has Nedd just lost us the game?

Taunts sound all around me as I stand on the sideline, copping the abuse of Bathurst supporters.

'Look what you've fucking done, kid!'

'You're fucked! You've ruined it for your whole team.'

My stomach twists into a knot as I watch the Bathurst kicker line up the penalty shot, now with just three minutes left on the clock. Is this it? Is this what our season will amount to? A penalty that sends Bathurst through to the final as we're forced to trudge to the locker room in silence, marinating in the melancholy that is defeat?

I force myself to watch as the kicker studies the posts, then begins his run-up. As the ball takes flight, I know. He's going to miss. There is a moment of quiet, then Forbes erupts.

Time runs out and the whistle blows and we can't leave the field as we huddle together, blowing hot air into one another's faces. We're going to the grand final.

There's a tap on a shoulder and our coach interrupts the celebrations, asking for quiet as he begins his speech to prepare us for the week ahead. Finishing up, he asks, 'Any niggles, boys?'

'Um, yeah,' I say, gesturing with my eyes to my knee, which has swollen to the size of my thigh.

He stares with disbelieving eyes, unsure how I managed to finish the game.

'Oh fuck, Nedd. Come here. Let's go,' he orders, hurrying me away for ice treatment that might start my recovery and have me right for next week.

A scan on the Tuesday reveals I've got prepatellar bursitis combined with a torn meniscus. The doctor explains that the former is an inflammation of the bursa in the front of the kneecap, something that occurs when it's shocked or irritated and responds by producing too much fluid.

His words drift in one ear and out the other. All I know is that I'm in agony and the swelling is putting pressure on other parts of the knee so that the whole area hurts to the touch. I tell the doctor about the grand final, pleading with him to help. When I ask what we can do for my knee ahead of the game, he lets out a long sigh.

'Shit, man,' he says, shaking his head. 'You can pray, but don't do it on your knees.'

I leave his clinic deflated, doubtful I'll be walking properly in a week let alone fit to play. But whether medicine can help or not, there's no debate here: *I have to play*. I've committed to this team and our goal of winning the premiership, and if doing my bit means playing on an angry bursa, then so be it.

ALL WEEK, I THINK about my team and what this final means to each of us. Time is running out to find a solution to my knee and despite my resolve to play, I find I'm panicking.

Logan messages me. Now living in Orange, he tells me he might have someone for me. Intrigued, I ask who that might be, but he doesn't let on. Days pass and I push any thought of getting help from my brother out of my head. Tomorrow is game day, and still my knee looks like there's a balloon beneath the flesh, threatening to pop at any moment. If it was going to settle down by itself, it would have happened by now. Time has run out, surely.

14

'Nedd, can you get to Orange now?'

Logan's tone is urgent. I can barely hear him over the hubbub of the players, who are in high spirits on the team bus, clambering over seats and yelling down the aisle as we await our departure. It's just gone 9 am and the morning light is still soft and pale. It seeps through the windows and illuminates the smiles on the faces of guys who can't quite believe we're headed to Orange to play the grand final.

I'd been debating whether to consult the Emus' sports doctor on arrival, but the team won't have it. Such things just aren't done, especially on game day. The only option we can think of at the eleventh hour is strapping the knee, swallowing a fistful of ibuprofen and hoping for the best. But Logan has other ideas.

'Nedd!' he yells.

I dig my phone into my ear, straining to hear him better, and there's no mistaking his words. 'You need to get here *now!*'

He may not have the best timing, but Logan always manages to come through. He's found someone to look at my knee, a retired doctor who used to play for Orange City, a team with a long-standing rivalry with the Emus. We may be advancing into enemy territory for the big match, but this doctor would like nothing more than to help out a team that might stand a chance of stealing victory from the Emus. The fact that I play for the Platypi is irrelevant, apparently – Logan says this guy will sort me out.

I quickly fill in my teammates on the plan, before hurrying off the bus to find my parents, trusting Mum to step on the gas and make good time on this mercy dash.

I should be focused on the game, running through various plays in my mind and visualising my kicking routine. But all I can think about is my knee and what this retired doctor might do to me.

It's 10:30 am when the family car pulls up outside the Orange Emus Rugby Club. In just a few hours the grandstand will be full and the ground littered with squashed beer cans. Already, the place is coming to life.

I see a lone figure standing by the changing rooms. As I approach, I take in the appearance of someone who looks like he's just stepped out of Birmingham after World War One. He's wearing a peaked cap and holding an Esky, over which his jacket has been delicately draped.

'Hello, Nedd,' he says in a friendly tone. 'Nice to meet you.'

I watch his eyes drift down to my knee. There's a momentary tightening of his features as he takes in the size of it. He nods, as though understanding his assignment, and his eyes return to mine.

'All right. Let's take a look at this knee.'

In the empty changing room, he examines my injury, feeling around the kneecap as I try to conceal my pain.

He makes the same diagnosis indicated by the scans, but rather than tell me to pray, he says he can inject the area to numb it for the duration of the match, allowing me to play pain-free.

He asks where the team and I are getting ready. I tell him about the pub we've booked out in Orange and he nods approvingly.

'Great,' he says. 'I'll see you there at 12:30.'

The boys sit around pub tables that are sticky from dried beer. We've already got our kit on and now it's just a matter of savouring these few moments of peace before kick-off. Some apply tape to various niggles, while others get a rubdown from the physio. Others still sip an electrolytes-infused beverage, their minds wandering from the pub to the oval down the road that beckons them.

When the doctor walks in with his Esky, which contains medical supplies, a hush falls over us.

'Do we know where Nedd Brockmann is?' the doc asks, his voice steady despite the adrenalised audience that sits before him, watching his every move.

As I walk towards him, his eyes dart about; he's searching for a clean space that might serve as a kind of operating room. The publican steps in and leads us upstairs to the staff bathroom, then blocks off the door as I set up the sports bed that I've borrowed from the team physio. I nervously sit down, watching as the doctor proceeds to take off his jacket, his trousers, and finally his shirt. Seeing the bewilderment in my wide eyes, he explains the disrobing.

'Hang on a minute, Nedd. I just need to get clean.'

Ready at last, he stands before me in singlet and boxer shorts. Momentarily, I wonder if this is all one big stitch-up, if Logan's about to come barrelling in, howling with laughter, camera in hand as he zooms in on my confused expression. But the minutes tick by and there's no punchline. I stretch my body flat on the sports bed as the doc takes out a tray of syringes, as well as some kind of fluid I can't identify.

'Right,' he says. 'We're going to replace all the fluid in your knee with anaesthetic.'

Before I can ask what that means, he inserts a needle into the bottom of my kneecap, while quickly positioning a steel tray below the injection site. Sure enough, a fluid – murky and tinged with blood – begins spilling out of my knee like water from a hose.

The door opens partially and I see Jack's face appear. He takes in my wild eyes and ashen complexion, the retired doctor hovering above me in his underwear, and the unholy vision that is the injection site. There's also blood smeared on my rugby socks and fluid spilling over the tray.

'Nedd, the bus is leaving,' he stutters. 'Do you want us to wait?'

The doctor answers on my behalf. 'Nedd will be with you shortly, Jack.'

'No worries,' says Jack, backing away from the door and closing it quickly, though not before I hear him gagging.

I watch as the doctor fills the same needle with anaesthetic and pushes it into my knee. When the procedure is complete, I expect to feel only a mild relief, but instead I feel reborn. It's as if nothing ever happened. More than that, it's as though I've been granted an upgrade, and I can now walk around with a new-and-improved model of kneecap.

Admittedly, the attire of boxer shorts and singlet had thrown me, but this man is a sage in my eyes. He's cured me.

'All right, Nedd,' he begins, 'you're going to be in a lot of pain as soon as you finish this game . . .'

There's more, but I don't hear anything else. His words bypass my ears and bounce off the walls, my mind already focused on the grand final and the job we have to do.

I rush to join all the boys on the bus, in socks stained red before the game has even begun. I can't feel any pain in my knee and as I give the thumbs-up to Jack, letting him know I'm back and raring to go, the doctor steps onto the bus. The chatter turns to silence – remarkable given he's still half-dressed. The doc's eyes move from one player to the next.

'Good luck today, boys,' he bellows.

And without so much as waiting for our excited cries in response, he walks off the bus and into the empty streets of Orange.

15

Looking at the crowd, I can't identify a single face. Features blur into one multicoloured swarm that intermittently erupts. It's either cheering loudly or protesting with outrage, but on the field it all sounds the same.

The Orange Emus jog onto the field with the complacent air of a team that's certain of victory. We've lost to them at our every meeting this season, most recently two weeks ago in the preliminary final. But that loss felt different to the earlier ones. We could all feel it. We were closer, the margin just a few measly points. And now, when everything's on the line, success feels possible. We're the underdogs and we're hungry. We can sniff victory and won't be satisfied with anything less.

The whistle blows and we go straight onto the front foot. There's no fumbling under big-match pressure, no easing into things. We seize opportunities and, within minutes, we're on the scoreboard thanks to a try.

Our lead is short-lived, though. The Emus respond with a play our defensive line can't stop and soon their supporters are jeering at us from the sidelines, buoyant with an inflated sense of superiority.

Throughout the match, the lead continues to change hands. It's back-and-forth, to-and-fro, such that when I catch sight of Mum and Dad in the grandstand, I detect the flush of nervous energy that stains their cheeks red.

With fifteen minutes to go, we're ahead by five points, 25-20. The yelling from the grandstand crashes into us like a wave as we receive a penalty within kicking distance. I tell Jack we should kick for goal. There's a flicker of doubt on his face as he considers my knee and the magnitude of the occasion. Should he really throw the ball to the injured youngster on the team and ask him to get the Platypi over the line? But my eyes display only confidence: *I can do this. I will get it done.*

'Do your thing, mate,' Jack commands, handing me the ball.

It'll need to be a 40-metre kick. Trying to place the kicking tee, I can't get it to lie flat. The ground has been butchered. The constant stampede of studded boots, back and forth, has kicked up great chunks of grass, leaving the surface pockmarked and uneven. I dig out some dirt and manage to set the tee evenly enough. I step out my approach and steady myself before the kick. As I look up at the goalposts, I can't help but smile. *This is it.* I should be nervous, taking such a crucial kick in front of so many eyes. But all I feel is a sense of calm. My mind knows it before my body has completed the action, as if I've already seen this scene unfold so many times behind closed eyes. *It's going through.*

The ball sails between the goalposts and is still in the air as I turn to the crowd, euphoric. My teammates rush up to me, smothering me in an embrace that leaves us all dizzy. I look at the scoreboard: 28–20. We just have to hold on.

We have to get through these remaining minutes, ideally without conceding another point.

Emu supporters are now watching anxiously, desperately. Their players feel the same way. Like a wounded animal, the team turns scrappy, trying anything and everything to get them over the line. But the clock is running down and we're not budging. When the final whistle blows, we can't quite believe what we've done.

'Is that it? Is that it?' we cry.

Everyone's jumping on one another. Beer spills from thrown cans with the lightness of a sprinkler. And before we can even embrace, we're engulfed in a sea of limbs as hundreds of people storm the field, celebrating what is a shared victory. Fourteen years it's been since Forbes have won a premiership, and here we are. To think I've been a part of something so extraordinary, and to have made friends for life in the process, is astounding. Even while it's happening, I know this is a moment I'll want to live in forever.

By the time the bus arrives back at the pub, most of the team are already half-cut and slurring their words. I can hardly sit down, acute pain now pressing against my knee as if trying to escape from beneath my skin. I'd played as if I'd been cured, forgetting that the doctor had warned me that the anaesthetic would wear off. Now that it has, walking is almost unbearable. Any slight bend in my leg causes a scream to escape my lips. The team are all downstairs singing songs, but as I enlist my arms to help get me up the stairs to my room, I know something is very wrong. I try to call Mum but she's already back at the farm, where reception is terrible. As soon as she picks up the phone, her voice breaks up before turning to static.

'Mum,' I text her, *'I need to go to the hospital.'*

I try and direct my mind to anything other than my knee, but such attempts are futile. It pulses with an intense discomfort with each breath. I hear my name being called, and when I gingerly make my way downstairs, I see Mum. She looks at the giant orb that's become my kneecap and tries to hide the horror that still flickers across her face. There's no time for deliberation. We just get into the car and drive.

At the hospital, we're greeted by a nurse whose eyes dart between Mum and me. She wants some detail about what I've done to myself.

'How did this happen?'

'Ahhh, not really sure,' answers Mum, her voice wavering slightly.

'Well, who was the doctor who did the injection?'

'Ummm, can't remember the name to be honest,' I say.

I can't bear to look at Mum, my cheeks flushed like a kid who's been caught with his hand in the cookie jar. The nurse seems to gather that my loyalties lie elsewhere, even if they've landed me in this mess, and with an eyeroll she ushers me through to emergency, where she pulls the curtains around a small bed that will be mine for the night.

When morning arrives, I'm discharged with a renewed diagnosis of prepatellar bursitis and a torn meniscus – and a knee so swollen it manages to turn heads as I walk out of the hospital and into the light. I was an idiot to play, apparently, but the damage isn't permanent.

It's not exactly the grand-final celebration I'd pictured, but even so I can't stop myself from smiling. I'm wearing it: a battle scar, a memento from this season and the match that sealed our fate, a tangible reminder of what it means to aspire to something and stop at nothing until it's achieved. It had been a struggle. Throughout the season, we'd had some tough games against strong opponents, but we'd never given up. Each week we returned to the field focused on the here and now but with the greater goal at the back of our mind. We stayed hungry, wanting to prove something to those who'd counted us out, but also to ourselves. You're never out of the fight. Even the biggest underdog may just have the power to win.

COME SEPTEMBER, FRIENDS from school have almost completed the first year of their degrees. Others have acquired jobs in their chosen field, ticking the first box in the long list that represents their career path and roadmap to life. I wonder if I should feel regret, or a feeling that I'm behind. Instead, all I feel is a keen sense that I've found myself, or at least that I'm getting closer to the person I want to be. This year, I committed myself to working on the farm with Dad and winning the premiership with Forbes, and in achieving both I've learned the power of words: they carry meaning when we back them with action.

But while it's one thing to win a premiership as part of a team when your whole town is behind you, it's another to show up every day, to do the work you must do, and to do it all alone, with no hope of praise or reward. My year on the farm with Dad has proved invaluable. In our early struggles to communicate, we learned the value of perspective – the need to consider things from another's point of view. Now, I no longer see a man who can't communicate, but rather one whose life has been lived quietly and diligently in service to his family. I see a man with a ticker no one could ever match, someone for whom quitting is never an option. In my dad, I see a body that withstands physical hardship and a temperament that never cracks; and in his heart I see a generosity without limits. I don't want to be a farmer, but I do want to live a life of service. I know that I want to work towards a greater purpose and, like Dad, help others to have opportunities in their lives that they'd otherwise lack. I don't yet know the path I will take to make this happen, but with Dad as my guide, I know I will get there.

16

It's only April, but already there's an uninviting chill in the air, as though winter has arrived early overnight. On such a morning, few things are as comforting as a warm bed, and the thought of burying myself deeper under the covers crosses my mind. But as I rub crumbs of sleep from my eyes, I regain my focus. I recall the desire I felt when I went to bed last night: the desire simply to run – further than I've ever run before.

In the darkness, I fumble around for my clothes: footy shorts, a rugby top, and training socks that I like to roll down to my ankles. I look at the only pair of trainers I have – so worn and tattered you can see the foam peeling away from the sole, sure to be lost on a lonely stretch of road in just a few strides. Look, they aren't ideal, but I hear people run barefoot these days, so surely a pair of worn-out trainers will be enough to get the job done. And besides, what's a few lost toenails if not all part of the process?

I step out the door and onto the driveway of the farm, sneaking a quick glance at my watch: 5:30 am, right on schedule. The sky looks like an unfinished watercolour, hues of pink and blue swirling through the murky purple of twilight. I won't get too sentimental about it, but it's a luxury to see the day take shape around you. Even the cattle seem contented as they graze under the cover of semi-darkness. Standing there in the eerie quiet, I feel like I'm taking hours from the day that aren't mine to take – a subtle act of thievery.

A momentary exhale before the world explodes once more into life. I look at the winding road leading out of the farm. And at the crossroads I've driven numerous times, on motorbike or tractor, all of them exploding with memories so that no corner doesn't elicit an emotion or release a flood of nostalgia from my youth. The feeling excites me. Everything familiar and yet in this moment, there's an uncertainty that gnaws at my bones. Time to get going.

I'm stiff at first, and for those early kilometres it feels as if my body is playing catch-up, perhaps frustrated by the early start and the demands forced upon it without notice. But I'm not waiting for anyone's permission. As I pick up the pace, I feel sleep's shadow fall away. A sense of rhythm envelops me, and I settle into it. Long strides, arms moving vigorously but relaxed, shoulders down, tall posture. It might just be the only time I've ever felt – dare I say it? – graceful. Having played footy for so long, where my eyes forever had to scan the field for a crafty opponent with a turn of speed or an unmatched goose step, I'm struck by how easy all this feels – this freedom to run without wariness or fear, without the need to glance over your shoulder every second to see whether someone might launch themselves at you like a human battering ram. To let your mind unfurl with each step, unencumbered by a coach's orders or the ticking of a clock.

Thoughts drift in and out. At times, I welcome them; other times, I reach for my phone and blare music to drown them out. Currently, they want to know what I'm made of, and what this running is all about. I don't have the answers, but I suppose that I will by the time I reach the local Woolworths, sixty kilometres away.

Right now, I'm aware only of my breathing and a sense of accumulating fatigue in my legs. With these trainers offering roughly the same amount of cushioning as a sheet of cardboard, I can feel a season's worth of summer heat baked into the tarmac. It licks at my heels like an invisible opponent, causing me to push off from the ground that little bit harder, only I never manage to pull away.

As I continue along that never-ending stretch of Bedgerabong road, light begins to slowly fill the sky and I wonder if this might be the start of my own morning ritual. To feel yourself alone like this, to sit in your own company with no interruption save the shriek of birds or some saccharine pop song bleeding out of a passing car radio . . . it's a gift. Free of obligation, driven only by my own determination, I feel like a kid who's just been freed from his parents' supervision, a sudden thrill of independence coupled with a keen sense of invincibility – the feeling that we might all be capable of achieving something simply because we're too naïve to believe otherwise, or haven't yet heard the negative voices that want only to bring us down. I can't explain it. I can only blink the sweat out of my eyes to know this is what it feels like to wake up and choose discomfort.

Nearing thirty kilometres, the screws come loose. The effortless, gazelle-like strides I had earlier are a distant memory, so too that feeling of invincibility. Now, it's pure survival mode, and I have the sinking feeling that mistakes have been made. What kind of an idiot heads out on a sixty-kilometre run with no water or nutrition? I shake my head just thinking of the ribbing I'll get from friends when I tell them what I've done. At various points of my body, it feels like sandpaper rubbing against brick, producing chafed skin that looks like the world's worst case of sunburn.

I remove my rugby top and tuck it into the waistband of my shorts, and just as I feel I'm descending into insanity, a car appears on the horizon at Jemalong. As though hallucinating, I see an outstretched arm waving from the driver's seat. It's Mum, bless her, once again saving the day with a bottle of water and a packet of Sour Patch Kids.

Do you know how good water tastes when you're practically drunk on dehydration? Do you know how exquisite? It's enough to convert even those who've acquired a taste only for sugar-laden soft drinks. Smooth on the palate, ice-cold. You'd swear you were drinking the finest quality H_2O, bottled and shipped express from Viti Levu. I gulp it down too quickly, and then regret not eating the Sour Patch Kids first as the sudden assault of citric acid and corn syrup leaves my throat dry and constricted. It's not exactly ideal nutrition for a feat of endurance, but the brain fog I had just moments ago is gone. I'm aware of my surroundings again, aware of what I set out to do.

And what was that exactly? To make it to Woolworths in five hours? It's an arbitrary marker of success. It's not so much the time I'm chasing as it is a feeling: the acute awareness of strain, a sense of effort that leaves you hollowed out and empty, save for that one voice in your head that gets louder. The voice that told you it could be done. Mum nods her encouragement and drives off to the destination, her car getting smaller and smaller on the horizon. All I can do is shuffle back out to the road where I tell myself to let it rip.

When I get to Woolworths, I lie down in the car park, but that's a mistake. The energy required to get back up isn't there. And the pain! I can't even put my arms down next to my body without feeling the sting of raw flesh. With legs that feel jammed at the kneecaps, I stagger to where I see Mum's parked car and stop my watch. Having covered those sixty kilometres, the time on my Garmin reads 4 hours 56 minutes.

A sense of accomplishment sweeps over me. It's less the time than the simple act of doing. The morning has barely begun and already I've pushed myself further than I thought possible. There was no opponent to chase down; no blue ribbon waiting at the finish line; no course record to break. Just a battle with my mind to dig deeper and never quit. It didn't fully hit me until that night, back in the warmth and comfort of my bed. To think every day henceforth could see me defy the limitations I have placed on myself, that every day I could show up as someone determined to silence the negative thoughts and prove the doubters wrong. Why wouldn't you steal those hours if you could? Why wouldn't you brace yourself for a challenge?

With heavy eyelids, I scan my room: everything unchanged, just as it was this morning. I don't know yet what the next challenge will be, but I understand from this day forward my life will be one spent in competition against myself – against the person I was yesterday and the unseen forces that threaten to keep me from my dreams. This night, I commit to choosing a life of challenges and struggle, if only to show others that anything is possible if you want it badly enough.

AFTER MY YEAR ON the farm with Dad and playing for the Forbes rugby team, I move to Canberra to study pharmacy at the University of Canberra. While pharmacy wasn't something I'd ever wanted to do or felt passionate about, when I got the marks for the course and then accepted into it, I sold the career to myself. They have a rugby team that I'm excited to play for, but in the second game I dislocate my shoulder making a tackle and need surgery. The surgeon manages to fix my shoulder well enough, but my days on the field are over. I find myself with time on my hands and no physical pursuit to direct it towards.

On campus, every Thursday evening marks the beginning of a long-weekend piss-up. I'm lost, searching, unsure what my purpose is and lacking any routine. When the year is up, I know I can't return unless I'm happy to settle one day into a job I don't care for. I'm also out of shape. I haven't picked up a weight or properly raised my heart rate for what feels like a lifetime. I see my future and it terrifies me: a dull job and sedentary lifestyle when what I crave is to use my mind and body. I decide to take up a trade, to get out of Canberra and relocate to Sydney, where I'll study to become an electrician.

17

My siblings and I were raised with the understanding that everyone is equal. You'd think this would be something preprogrammed into the brains of humans, but chances are you've encountered enough people by now to know otherwise.

We were free to steer our own course in life, to make our own decisions, whether they were guided by passion, ambition or the kind of lofty goals only a teen would harbour until reality intrudes. I know we are privileged to have this luxury of choice, but I can't always make sense of it. I find myself grappling with questions around my good fortune: how did I get so lucky to have parents committed to my well-being and happiness, parents who provided a permanent safety net beneath me.

These kinds of questions accost me when I settle in Sydney to study electrotechnology. My morning walk to the TAFE at Ultimo, on the southern fringe of Sydney's CBD, takes me along Eddy Avenue, where city traffic squeezes through narrow streets against an incessant soundtrack of aggressive honks and obscenities yelled from open windows, while litter overflows from bus-stop rubbish bins.

One morning, I should be running to class but the scenes around me demand I stop. Homeless folk crowd along the footpath, seeking refuge in warm pockets of Central Station, where the heat from the coffee shops and bakeries grants temporary relief from the cold.

It's not as though I've never seen a homeless person before, but you can't compare a country town with a sprawling city like Sydney. Here, their struggles are as tangible as the few possessions they squat alongside: a half-empty suitcase, a stained blanket – a life downsized to fit in a banged-up milkcrate.

What I'm seeing all but paralyses me. I don't know what to do or how to help. I watch as suits barrel unseeing along the footpath, sidestepping the homeless like potholes. I watch as those in need search for a set of eyes to connect with, only for faces to turn downwards and away. I watch how easy it is to ignore an outstretched hand, to turn a blind eye to suffering, to prioritise your own immediate needs while forgetting what it means to be human.

I tell myself to do something, to act on the feeling stirring inside me, willing me to give back and find a way to help – no matter how small the impact. So, I walk over and sit down next to one of my fellow men. The skin of his face bears the flush of sunburn, raw and cracked around his lips and nose. His matted hair forms dreadlocks that frame searching eyes, and while he hesitates to meet my gaze, slowly he begins to open up. Conversation flows between us, and he tells me his name is Dave. And when he does – when he speaks his own name – he shifts and stretches in his sleeping bag as if the mere hearing of it allows him to take up space without shame.

Thereafter, I spend hours doing this before and after class every Tuesday – conversing with someone sleeping rough on the streets. To those shivering from cold, I offer a hoodie. To others, I give food and hot coffee. But most often, what they really want is the chance to talk to someone who affords them a little respect without judgment. I learn that regardless of how long someone's been marginalised, the need for connection never leaves. It simply lies dormant, ready to awaken before a receptive stranger.

To sit with our society's most forlorn and hear their stories is to realise how little we know. News reports reduce the homeless to statistics referenced in the same breath as alcoholism and drug use. We ignore the fact that anyone's personal circumstances can change abruptly. We prefer to blame the victim for bad choices and personal failures. We tend not to consider other possibilities, like an escape from domestic violence, sudden unemployment, unpayable medical bills, eviction. I have a safety net. Not everyone does.

Seeing the fear in the faces of the homeless (*Where will I sleep tonight? Where is my next meal coming from?*), I vow not to forget their plight. I do some research, read up on the statistics: roughly one in 200 Australians sleep rough. Young people aged 15–24 make up twenty-one per cent of the homeless population, though older women appear to be the fastest-growing at-risk demographic. And these figures are likely to be the tip of the iceberg.

No amount of food or free clothing will be enough. And the issue sure as hell can't be fixed by one guy spending a few hours a week chatting and handing out a coffee. I'm not the answer, I know, but in some small way I'm going to make a difference. I want people to care deeply about others, like my mum and dad do.

I START EARNING MONEY as an apprentice sparkie, making $12.50 an hour in my first year. The pay is low, but the hours are structured, which I like. As I do more jobs around Sydney, I see people out training, shadow boxing in dimly lit parks and doing push-ups in those outdoor fitness playgrounds. Part of me wants to join them, but my priority is work. I'm paying $300 a week in rent for a room in a share house in Randwick. Calling this place an 'apartment' would be a stretch. With no balcony or green space, it's more like a dogbox, with paint flaking from the walls. Nonetheless, the rent is consuming most of my paycheque, to the point that a gym membership is out of the question. In the supermarket, I scan the aisles for specials. My stock meal becomes tinned tuna atop a mound of white rice.

I hate being unfit. Since I stopped playing rugby, I've done hardly any training. I've traded evenings in the gym for nights in dimly lit pubs, going round-for-round with the lads before crawling into bed with fingers still coated in oil and salt from the hangover cure-all of fried chicken and chips. In the same way that being consistent with your training adds up, so too do the excess kilos on my expanding frame from the nights of swallowing booze and eating like crap.

When I look in the mirror, I see a body symbolic of the way my life is heading. I've never really been self-conscious about my body before, but I feel it now as I observe skin slack against muscles lacking all tone and a bloated stomach. I miss the defined, sinewy physique I'd chiselled in my rowing and rugby days.

In Sydney, though, most people seemed to be active. You see them in the mornings, jogging along narrow streets or doing pull-ups in parks. Theirs is a collective desire to better themselves, physically and mentally. I know I need some kind of structure back in my life. It's time to do something about this beer belly.

One day, I finish work and commit to action, lacing up my trainers and heading out for a run. I cover just one-and-a-half kilometres before I turn around, cheeks red, sweat pouring off me, struggling to fill my lungs with oxygen. I need to walk back, but I know this is just the start.

The next day I go again and make it that little bit further. The next week, I go for five kilometres, then ten, and so on until I reach a marathon distance. I don't care anymore about my weight, and the running never gets much easier. But the completion of each run feels like a personal victory that inspires me to push further.

18

That sixty-kilometre run had brought everything into focus. I know this is it, that I want to test my limits. I want to end each day lying in bed as I had that night back at the farm, my body wrung out like a human rag, muscle fibres trying desperately to repair themselves, all while a sense of euphoria settles over me like a blanket, finally bringing stillness to my overactive mind.

It's funny how quickly you forget about the pain of calloused heels, lost toenails and bloodied nipples raw from chafing. I can still feel the ridges of blisters now dried out, but the agony of that run is a mere footnote to a bigger story. We don't give our bodies enough credit for their ability to withstand and heal pain.

My alarm gets set for 4 am, but it's an unnecessary precaution. Most mornings I'm up and about, shoes tied, pounding the street by 3:30, screaming at the top of my lungs to no one. I run ten kilometres, making it back with just enough time to shower and swallow some coffee before heading to a construction site for a day on the tools.

I'm a sponge ready to absorb all the information I can from those who've chosen the kind of path I imagine for myself; those who've turned their back on the stability that comes with a secure job that nonetheless fails to ignite their passions. Some of these inspirational figures are endurance athletes, but most are just ordinary people with a renegade spirit, people prepared to venture into uncharted territory because they relish the unknown.

I commit myself to American entrepreneur Andy Frisella's '75 Hard' challenge, which is seventy-five consecutive days where you have to: do two forty-five-minute training sessions, one of which has to be performed outside; consume no alcohol and stick to a predetermined diet with no cheat meals; read at least ten pages of a nonfiction book; drink 3.5 litres of water; take progress photos. I choose to run in the morning and do a strength session in the evening. Meanwhile, as an on-site apprentice, I discover most of the physical labour falls on my shoulders. I'm chasing walls with concrete cutters, operating the jackhammer, contorting myself to squeeze into the claustrophobia-inducing hollow of a roof, and crawling around on floors. The frequent inhalation of dust leaves me dizzy with a pounding headache between my eyes, but even on those days when I want nothing more than to go home and flop on the couch, I stick with the program.

I think of Dad working on the farm. He never voiced one complaint, nor did he ever hit snooze on the alarm to grant himself the sleep-in he deserved. He simply put one foot in front of the other and got on with the job for the sake of us, the family snoring their heads off back at the house. Arriving home after a sixteen-hour day coated in dried concrete and grime isn't exactly the breeding ground for motivation, but

Dad would never throw in the towel, so why would I? On those days when it felt like each step was a battle between body and mind and the only thing keeping me going was willpower, I thought of the man who raised me.

I have no coach, no training schedule, no looming race or competition I have to train for. There is nothing holding me accountable except my own word, and to me that is binding. When I resolve to achieve something, I don't do so like the child who's told in one breath to dream big and in another to make sure they have a safety net in place. Forget the net. I will get it done or die trying.

That's why I can't keep my eyelids closed a minute longer. An excitement churns in my stomach that I can't ignore. It's 11 pm on a Friday, and I know sleep won't come. So, I make a decision: I'll run 100 kilometres to Palm Beach and back through the night. Before I can talk myself out of it, I'm out the door with a backpack containing a bottle of Gatorade, three Cliff Bars and a muffin. Should be sweet, right?

The weekend is just beginning for revellers on Sydney's Oxford Street. Running under a glow of fluorescent light, I feel the pulse of club music blaring from open doors, from which drifts the aroma of stale beer and sweat. Stragglers mill about on the footpath, creating their own dance parties in the wake of exclusion, kicked out or refused another round of drinks. Their bodies are slack and loose, limbs flailing, free of inhibition. I smile as I run past and utter a 'How ya going?' between breaths. The stragglers look momentarily confused, before taking stock of my backpack and running attire and realising this is just some unhinged bloke doing something crazy in the middle of the night.

None of these guys has any idea of what I'm about to go through, I think. And a laugh escapes from my throat.

Life is a series of choices. Doors open and you're beckoned to follow a certain path. In this moment, I can't imagine any other path than the one I'm running.

When I reach Palm Beach at 3 am, I've downed the Gatorade, eaten all three Cliff Bars and have just twelve per cent battery remaining on my phone. I can barely see the outline of buildings against the blackness of the sky, let alone some kind of scenic view. So, I turn around almost immediately and begin the fifty-kilometre return journey. By the time I get home, my body is in a world of pain. I can feel the ripple of tendons beneath skin. An invisible force seems to be jamming into my hip socket with each step and my feet feel like two sodden cucumbers being pressed into shards of glass. I clamber into a cold shower, after which I barely have the energy to dry off. I have about as much control over my body as those I passed on Oxford Street hours earlier. My back seizes up as I stretch out on my mattress at 9 am, but I feel euphoria knocking on my door once more, a feeling of pure bliss, powerful enough to bury this pain like a bone somewhere in the deepest recesses of my mind.

Sleep descends . . . but not for long. The thrill of personal victory carries me like a buoy in high tide, and I'm jolted awake by a mind that wants direction, that wants to know what I can do next to make me feel this way again. When I call Mum the next day, I already have the answer.

'I'm going to run fifty marathons in fifty days,' I tell her.

Mum doesn't so much as miss a beat. 'Great, honey. How are you going to do that and can we help?'

That's the thing about my mum: she knows that once I've voiced a plan, I'm going to work wholeheartedly to see it happen. So, rather than respond with negativity or concern, she instead wants only to help me think through the practicalities and make herself useful. Sometimes I don't think she realises that just hearing the validation in her response is enough. Her voice – the voice of reason – never questioning my desire for the extreme.

19

An American ultramarathoner by the name of Dean Karnazes had already run fifty marathons (42.195 kilometres), covering the fifty US states in fifty days. The premise of it was simple enough, though not one I can latch onto in Australia. Needing my own point of difference, I figure I can keep things interesting by working as an apprentice throughout the whole endeavour. A marathon every day for fifty days, all while spending at least eight hours every day on my feet, doing whatever manual labour is required of me.

It's a challenge that keeps me awake nights, my body fired up at the prospect of proving itself once more.

After speaking to Mum on the phone, I announce my intentions to the world in a social-media post. It's a way of formalising an agreement I've now made with myself. I know I will show up each day until those fifty marathons are done, even if I'm crawling by the end of it.

The doubters come at me with the aggression of sharks at feeding hour. 'No chance, mate,' they say. Others favour the use of expletives as they suggest I rejoin reality.

At first blush, the plan does seem outlandish, particularly when you consider my running resume, which suggests more inexperience than a recent university grad trying to bluff their way through a job interview. That said, in the space of three months, I've gone from being a reluctant hobby jogger to someone who's completed a sixty-, then eighty-kilometre run, before taking on 100 kilometres with little more than the kind of unwavering enthusiasm you'd expect of a kid come Christmas morning. I look in the mirror and see a physique that's hardening up again, but I still don't see myself as a runner per se. I'm not chasing a record, not even a personal best, or an audience on Strava. I'm just doing what I've set out to do since that morning run in Forbes. *Choose life every day, squeeze from it what you can.*

Something else, too. I'm going to raise money for the homeless and create as much awareness around the issue as I can. Everyone has a 'why' – the reason you trade the comfort of a warm bed for grey skies and freezing winds, evenings on the couch for hard sessions that leave you spent. I can't think of a greater purpose than this.

Supporters suggest I need more time. They offer to write up training plans replete with weekly mileages and incremental increases, all designed to get my legs used to repetitive strain and little rest. I don't want to hear it, though, especially if it means a delayed start. I once heard someone make the off-hand comment that 'if it's not a broken bone, you can run on it'. And I took that as gospel. Every other issue can be overcome.

Can you ever, truly prepare your body for a fifty-in-fifty? I suspect not. Too much can go wrong, and every run carries with it a sense of uncertainty. How will your stomach respond to whatever fuel you gave it today? How much sleep did you manage to clock the night before? And then there's the sudden onslaught of thoughts – fears, really – that you can no longer compartmentalise or ignore. But that's also what keeps it interesting: you never know for sure what each run holds or who you'll be at the end of it.

So yes, there are unknowns; yes, there are variables, but you can, mostly, control your own mind. I may not have put multiple marathons back-to-back before, but I had made a habit of banking twice-daily sessions, for no reason other than I'd promised myself I would. To get this done, I knew, my mind was the only tool I'd need.

WAKING ON THE MORNING of 31 August 2020, no part of me doubts my ability to complete the fifty-day challenge. I relish the sound of the 5 am alarm because it means I can finally start.

I'd expected that my days at work would pass as normal – yes, muscles straining under the weight of various loads and lungs wheezing from all the concrete dust I inhale like second-hand smoke, but no great mental challenges to confront. I was wrong.

All I can think about by day is the grim reality of what awaits me upon the instruction of 'tools down': the next run – and this constant battle with my body: post-work, I'm required to keep it moving for another four hours or so; that's the deal.

The guys onsite are quick to offer their assistance whenever I need a sparring partner in the afternoon to keep my energy levels up. But as soon as I leave and join the slow-moving traffic of the post-work commute, I am locked in a torturous game of mental arithmetic. I begin counting the minutes it'll take me to get home and change, and calculating what time it'll be when I finally start running, how a later finish will impact that night's recovery, and how long it will take me to cook dinner and get something down before bed, all with the understanding that no matter how out of sync I get, the whole process starts again tomorrow.

The first week is punishing. Each morning I rise hesitantly, my legs dangling off the bed with all the grace of a flat tyre, heavy and deformed from inflammation. I look down at swollen toes and tentatively begin placing my weight on my angry, overworked feet. Each morning, I expect calamity. I feel like something will snap at any moment. But as the morning hours pass and I have no choice but to execute various tasks, it begins to feel as though my muscles are crawling out of a deep slumber. I'm no sports doctor, but I realise that tendons do actually warm up, that despite all the stiffness and cramps and soreness, all I have to do is just break into a shuffle and let muscle memory kick in.

And then, twelve days in, disaster strikes. There's a sudden sting in my right hamstring, as though a bowling bowl has been set alight and is thundering up my leg, burning its way up to my rump. My breath catches and I emit a scream that could rip open a man's chest. I check my Garmin and my stomach sinks: I'm just eight kilometres into this run, with another thirty-four to go. I want to crawl off into the bushes and hide like some wounded animal, all sense of pride steamrolled by this reminder of my own fallibility. But as quickly as those thoughts flood in, so too does my resolve. It cuts through the noise and gets me problem-solving. I take a stride on my right: agony, like my glute muscle might tear off the bone. I take a shortened stride: hmmm, tolerable. I can work with that.

There is no switching off, no mental happy place I can check into to get me painlessly through those thirty-four kilometres. With each half-stride on my right leg, I feel a stabbing pain in my hamstring, which responds by quivering in fright. The sound coming in through my AirPods is drowned out by my own screams, while sweat mixes with tears to create a salty paste on my face.

By the time I finish the run, I am empty, too drained to panic at the sight of the ice bath, too tired to ponder what will become of the injury in the days and weeks ahead. All I do is remember what I take to be axiomatic: *if it's not broken, you can run on it*. And with the comfort of knowing my injury is not a break but just a tear, I drift off to sleep. Tomorrow is a new day.

I KNOW IF I CAN get to ten days, I'll get to fifty. I know if I can just keep showing up, I'll finish what I've started.

More issues do arise, of course. I tear calves and quads, and some days I can barely get my trainers tied due to the swelling in my Achilles tendons. Every part of my body feels as though it's been directly in the firing line. It's a feeling beyond fatigue. Like faulty wiring that could short-circuit and blow at any moment, I am a walking safety hazard. And yet I'm still here, proving the doubters wrong. In my mind, I can't be stopped.

I think of the people I'd met on the streets, sleeping on benches or mattresses fashioned out of discarded boxes and sheets of cardboard. People whose only source of warmth in winter was a garbage bag and newspaper they draped over their body like a sheet. They seemed to inhabit a permanent state of discomfort.

By contrast, no matter how sore my legs or how busted my feet, my pains are temporary. I can finish my run and head back to a hot shower and warm meal. I can stretch out my body on a foam mattress under a roof and know exactly when my next paycheque is coming and how much I'll receive and what it will buy me. If there was any fear I felt in regard to how my body might function the next day, it was nothing compared to the fears and uncertainties of those sleeping rough.

For the final run, on 19 October, Mum and Dad leave the farm and come to Sydney to see me finish. And with each lap of Centennial Park, where I've run most of my marathons during the past seven weeks, I can hear Dad's cries of encouragement. Footpaths that are normally dotted with runners and dog-walkers are instead swarming with people whose faces blur into one. I see hands extended towards me, phones held aloft, everyone trying to capture a feeling.

The completion of each run leading up to this final marathon had seen me suppress any building sense of satisfaction. For me, each run was just another box to be checked off somewhere deep in my skeletal system, a precursor to the nightly ice bath and carb-load that had become routine. But as the GPS ticks over to 42.195 kilometres on this, marathon No. 50, the emotional floodgates open.

Towards the end, I've no longer had the vocabulary to describe the suffering I've endured. And I've found a sense of power in that – to have sat with discomfort and stared down defeat, to have given both the middle finger.

The end brings a rush of joy beyond anything I've ever known. Though the triumph feels deeply personal, it's one I can share with others because they have some understanding of the depths I've plumbed.

Here in Centennial Park, I look at Mum and Dad through a fog of tears. Both are beaming with pride, though their expressions contain no trace of the surprise I see on the faces of the strangers who surround me. My parents: two people who know better than anyone how my mind works. Two people who taught those lessons on never giving up, no matter the cost. Why would they be surprised? They knew before I did that if I were to set my mind to something, I'd achieve it.

20

When you've trained your mind to run through untold pain, you begin to tempt fate. I feel untouchable, like there is no physical challenge that's beyond me. I give myself three days to savour the sense of accomplishment I feel at having completed those fifty marathons, before returning to the daily grind of logging miles in the dusk. Two weeks later, I'm running 200 laps of the Bronte hill loop – a loop that drives you crazy not from repetition but the incline that greets you like a sheer cliff face.

I am running alone, but there's an audience of sorts. It seems like those who'd once doubted my abilities are in my corner now, looking for the bleached mullet to chase down. I am getting messages from people who've started their own fitness journey, individuals who've tossed in their job to pursue their passion instead.

It feels like all eyes are on me, that people are waiting for the announcement of my next crazy endeavour, or for a Strava upload in which the kilometres hit triple digits. Somehow, I've found an audience that, far from being repulsed by my extreme deeds, wants to celebrate them, an audience that encourages me to dream bigger, go bolder, run further. And like a born performer, I want to give them what they crave, to inspire them the only way I know how: by *doing*. There's just one problem: the doing is becoming unbearable.

Something's wrong with my right IT (iliotibial) band – the thick band of fibrous tissue that runs along the outside of your leg. Even before the pain became impossible to ignore, I knew it. At first it felt like my knee was just locking up, an unpleasant sensation suggesting cartilage rubbing against bone. I kept running through that. Then the feeling was like a jackhammer to the thigh, right along the length of it. I kept running through that, too. Now, my knee has swollen to the size of a rockmelon and every step hurts like a parking ticket.

I reluctantly visit my physio, Belly, hoping a few sessions will settle the knee and have me running freely again. But then I hear two words – 'irreversible damage' – and my eyes glaze over.

Belly is outlining the surgery required and the rehab plan to follow, and yet I can't make sense of his words. Aren't I meant to be invincible? Isn't that what I've proven?

My mind wanders.

I didn't set out on those fifty marathons thinking people would pay much attention to the madman with a face taut from clenching his jaw to stifle the obscenities he wanted to scream. But with each marathon, more people would join me on those laps around Centennial Park. They were runners and friends, strangers and exercise enthusiasts, all of them inspired to start doing something for no reward or recognition, but because it might just make them a better person or allow them to see more clearly what life's about. For the most part, they trotted behind or to the side of me, careful not to get in my way.

At some point, I knocked elbows with a guy named Tom and heard a British accent thick enough to spread on toast. Later, I'd learn that, as an eighteen-year-old, Tom had run from the top to the bottom of the United Kingdom, averaging some fifty-three kilometres per day for a month. He was an extremist by nature, someone who relished the opportunity to enter the Pain Cave because he knew that to emerge was to discover you were capable of more than you thought.

Tom had caught wind of my endeavour and felt a certain kinship with me: two guys whose shared instinct is to attack the impossible. The first time he joined me on one of my marathon runs, we simply exchanged pleasantries. But it soon became clear to me that Tom wasn't interested in small talk. This was a guy who approached friendship with the same reverence he approached life. He was someone who'd show up for you and want to know exactly the depth of your suffering, if only to remind you of the lows you'd felt and conquered before.

I start to hear Belly again. And my path becomes clear, and hopefully manageable.

After the surgery to treat the IT-band friction syndrome that had been plaguing my right leg, I'm in a moon boot, staring down five months of inactivity before I can even think about starting a rehab program. I'd held the future I'd imagined for myself like sand between my fingers, and each day it seems to be slipping away with greater speed.

No part of me wants to return to life as a tradie, not because there's anything wrong with the work but because my heart isn't in it. Having experienced the euphoria of completing those runs, I'm drawn towards a life of challenge. I need a purpose, a cause – a good one in which others can share.

Incapacity has left me feeling lost, directionless. When I meet Tom at the Coogee Pavilion on 12 December 2020 for a drink and a chicken parmi, it's partly to seek his guidance. My certainty of recent months has gone, ripped off me like a cape, and suddenly I'm questioning whether I'm made of the right stuff. But Tom won't let me entertain these doubts. He reminds me that my superpower has never been about physical strength, but rather the tool I've leaned on time and again: my mind.

I look at him then and, without realising just how much I'd been thinking about it, I float an idea that had come to me midway through the fifty marathons. How about this: I run across Australia, some 4000 kilometres, where I knock off an average 100 kilometres per day, with the aim of completing the journey in 43 days, faster than anyone's ever done it as far as we know?

Tom doesn't bat an eyelid. He asks when I'll be starting.

Not that I need his approval, but in Tom I've found a comrade in battle. Between us we have our own verbal shorthand based on a mutual understanding of extreme, largely self-inflicted physical suffering of such intensity that to describe it to others – or to try to – would convince them you're crazy. Tom understands what it will take to complete the journey I'm proposing and how it will test and break open my psyche to a point where I'll never be quite the same again. In voicing my desire to run across the country, I know immediately that Tom will be in my corner. No matter how dark things get, he'll be rooting for me from the get-go.

Six months pass before I get the doctor's go-ahead to set off on a slow jog. But with the prospect of another mighty challenge filling my head, small victories like this are like lemonade in the desert. While running is off limits, I find ways to push myself in the gym by targeting upper-body strength. I also seek out the great teachers of endurance, those who've scaled tremendous heights not for any reward but to challenge the status quo and truly to *live* every hour, not just let another one tick by.

I spend time back at the farm, connecting with family and friends, trying to show up for others in the same way Tom has for me. And in these six months when my GPS watch sits inactive, I'm reminded that the run I'm planning is a vehicle, not my raison d'être. Because I'm not a runner. I'm someone who uses the sport to test myself, not to define my self-worth. I will not let it do that. And just as I'd approached the fifty marathons with tenacity and enthusiasm, I handle those months laid up in the same way. This is who I am: Nedd, someone who has time for people, someone who won't let down himself or anyone else. People didn't connect with me because I'd run fifty marathons. They connected with me because I'd made them feel less alone – and more connected to their dreams.

People like Tom are hard to find. More common are people who'll tell you all the reasons why you can't do something, rather than the reasons why you should. I'm not going to let an injury bring me down. I'm still going to set myself to achieve things that others regard as impossible. And this time, I'll know better the man who's doing it.

PART THREE: BIGGER THAN THE RECORD

It's about choosing to live life to the full, knowing nothing is guaranteed, that it can all be snatched away in an instant.

Nedd

21

The fatigue of fifty marathons has barely left my legs when management companies begin coming to me with offers. Though my purpose had only ever been to push beyond self-imposed limits and raise money for the homelessness charity, We Are Mobilise, somehow I've been classified as a marketable product. Noting my bleached mullet and laidback attitude, commercial types get dollar signs in their eyes. Contracts arrive at my door, littered with legal jargon and figures I can't make sense of.

Some youngsters are bred for athletic performance and success. They have a tennis racquet or golf club thrust into their hands before they've learned to recite the alphabet and, consequently, if they're exceptionally talented and lucky too, theirs is a future of national championships, sports agents and lucrative endorsements. But when you're a 21-year-old tradie still rushing off to work at six in the morning to screw light fittings to walls for twenty bucks an hour, such a future seems way out of reach. I can understand how my story might capture people's attention, and why this desire to push yourself might prove contagious. But suddenly to be branded an influencer? I can't wrap my head around it.

I'm not a brand to be sold or a cog in a profit-making machine. I'll define success in my own terms and won't trade my integrity for fame and a flash car.

The companies targeting me try to push me into a corner. They see a quick cash-grab in the form of a kid who doesn't know what to make of the sudden attention his feats of endurance have attracted. I see their motive clearly: they want to make bank, fast. And they care little, if it all, for me or what I'm about.

Though perhaps there's an exception in the mix.

It's a family friend who introduces me to James Ward, who earlier in 2020 had cofounded Bursty, a sports-focused marketing agency that seeks to connect athletes with audiences around the world through powerful storytelling and purpose-driven collaborations. He's been in the management and marketing game for some time but is looking for a greater purpose. He wants to tell stories about people who have the power to make a difference.

The first time we speak, James thinks I was merely trying to capitalise on the success of the fifty marathons.

'Is that it,' he asked, 'or are you planning on doing something else?'

'I want to run across Australia in 43 days and 12 hours to break the current world record,' I told him. 'Oh, and also raise a million dollars for homelessness.'

I expect an eyeroll that you could measure on the Richter Scale. Instead, James utters five words: 'I can make that happen.'

When we connect, it's as two guys wanting to create magic. I feel like I've found someone on the same wavelength, someone driven to leave the world in better shape than it's in now.

With James, money is an afterthought. The goal is not a sum to be amassed but rather the opportunities that could be created along the way. James wants to use his connections to help me make a difference on a bigger scale than I've managed so far.

SINCE RAISING WITH TOM the idea of running across Australia, the enormity of the task has been eating away at me. My days spent on construction sites increasingly feel like a grind and a source of agitation because I'm not doing what excites me. Hours become days, days become weeks and still I'm stuck chasing concrete walls for the security of a paycheque.

I have some sense, I think, of the physical demands the run will put on me, but the operation's logistics are like a foreign language. I don't know where to start or what will be required. James can see it's going to be costly – even just fuelling the support van that will be charting the route alongside me will be a whopping expense. He knows we'll need sponsors to get behind the challenge, if only to get the word out and help raise more money along the way. He puts out feelers, hits up and makes contacts, and lines up meetings. I sit down with shoe companies and entrepreneurs that have zero belief in my capacity to do what I propose. Most laugh, while others sit in stunned silence, as if waiting for the mask of confidence they think I'm wearing to slip off and reveal something fragile or deranged.

They don't seem to realise that the man they're sitting opposite is not an athlete with extensive media training who's worried about displaying any vulnerability. The man they're sitting opposite is just me, an open book. Perhaps they underestimate what I'm capable of, figuring I'd maxed out with the fifty marathons and will never be able to extract so much from my body again. But I'm simply telling the truth. I *will* run across Australia. I'm not trying to be someone I'm not or to come across in a certain way.

Since I first thought of it, the cross-country run has sunk its claws into my skin like a parasite. I'm now in the grip of a fever-dream, unable to think of anything else. I sit before powerful people with no sense of fear or intimidation, with no façade to maintain. My heart is in it, I'm invested, and I will make it happen. Even so, my assurances are falling on deaf ears.

'Yeah, cool,' is the typical response, delivered with faux enthusiasm. Phone calls and follow-up meetings are promised but never transpire. As the months pass and still no sponsors are onboard, I can sense James' belief in the run starting to wane.

Is my latest dream more like a pipedream? And never mind the dearth of sponsors – is it even physically possible? I awake each day consumed with the dread of what it might feel like to be running on empty two weeks into a month-long epic. I want to know what such an eventuality could mean for your body and mind. Would it be possible to come back from that – from the insanity that surely takes hold of someone in the grip of mental and physical exhaustion?

They were questions few had dared to ponder and even fewer knew the answers to. I was determined to find out for myself.

22

I'm out of the moon boot and throwing everything I have into my training. I know what peak fitness feels like and refuse to settle for a body that isn't willing or able to go the distance and stay in the fight.

The COVID-19 pandemic has seized the world and, in lockdown, parks and footpaths that were once teeming with exercisers are now all but empty, as are the calendars for big-time sport.

For many, the pandemic is cause to question why they've been doing certain things. What, for example, is the point of training if the world as we know it has disappeared? Is it worth the sacrifice of early mornings spent in the elements, under grey skies and lashing winds?

Some give up their exercise completely, trading it for the comfort of a warm bed and a leisurely breakfast. But another group relishes the opportunity to step up the physical training, not because a big match or competition is approaching (they're all cancelled) but because it's in a state of exertion that one feels most alive. In case it's not clear by now, I belong to this second group.

You can't help who you are, and when I get back into running, I do so with the mindset of a man who'd once thought himself invincible. It isn't long before a stress fracture appears in my shin. So, what to do? The gym becomes a second home where I focus all my attention on getting as strong as possible. There are no biceps curls performed in front of a mirror, no flexes for the 'gram. Rather, I commit to all-out sweat sessions, thirty minutes of high-intensity, full-body exercises that leave me feeling like a piñata at a kid's birthday party. These workouts don't provide me with quite the same sense of escape as running does, but they do allow me to feel like I'm in control of my fitness and restore the satisfaction inherent in meeting daily commitments.

Nonetheless, when you're eyeing up a 4000-kilometre journey across Australia on foot and urgently seeking sponsors to back you, the last thing they want to hear is that you've got a stress fracture in a leg. James is inclined towards keeping the injury inhouse. Soon, however, the meetings become more sporadic, and weeks pass in which James and I don't talk, both of us seemingly doubting the other's capacity to uphold his end of the bargain.

I feel like I'm treading water, barely able to keep my head above the surface long enough to breathe. I'm getting nowhere. Days pass with little to differentiate them from the one before and I can feel my frustration mounting. But it's always darkest before the dawn.

The strength training helps keep me sane and I gradually increase my running mileage. I'm running better, too. It feels like I've finally made the leap from the cautious steps of a wounded runner to the confident strides of one who's confident in his body and knows it's capable of producing a burst of speed on request. It is time to start making things happen. It is time to go.

James is taking the Hume Highway to Wagga Wagga when I call him. We go back and forth, trading barbs over the lack of sponsors. I hear the *click click click* of an indicator over the line as James pulls over, too tense from our conversation to keep driving.

Where I'm at, I don't care if the run leaves me out of pocket and becomes a cowboy operation and logistical nightmare. I know I cannot go another month without a confirmed start date. I need clarity on this, and I'm not prepared to keep pushing things back indefinitely because of some arbitrary checklist.

'James, we have to put our balls on the line here and go with it, otherwise we're just going to keep dancing around,' I say. 'There's never going to be a right time to start. We've just got to *start*.'

James's breathing comes out in staccato-like bursts. I can hear the annoyance in his sighs. Here he is, dealing with some kid who wants to run across Australia with no idea what that will involve. Heck, even I can understand why he's getting so frustrated with me. But while James is filled with doubt, I'm still nothing besides confident.

'If it's meant to be, we'll get sponsors,' I say. 'And my determination to keep showing up and see it through will make this happen. But I'm going to stop talking about it because it's chewing me up. It's consuming me. I'll get it done.'

'Righto,' James says, before hanging up.

IT HAD BEEN NERVE-RACKING announcing the fifty marathons to the world. As soon as I went public with it, I knew there was a job to do, and thereafter my every waking thought went towards making it happen. Now, I'm facing an even bigger challenge, and as soon as I put it out there in the form of an Instagram post, I feel an immediate hardening of purpose. I am no longer drifting. Days aren't simply passing by. I am working towards something, showing up for myself and the person I want to become. Once it's out there, you have a date and you have to honour it, no matter what obstacles get in your way.

23

I'm still clocking eight-hour days onsite, roughing in kitchens, fitting off lights and doing whatever else needs doing. It scares me, the ease at which you could let things slide on, waiting for that next thing to come along, thinking you need to have all your ducks in a row before you pursue it.

But as I said to James, there is never going to be a perfect time to start this run, nor am I ever going to reach a level of fitness that would ease the anxiety involved in preparing for a 4000-kilometre effort. I leap into the unknown and invite others to follow me. A daring few do.

It's been all quiet on the sponsorship front when James and I meet with Adam Linforth of swimwear company Budgy Smuggler. I've been speaking on podcasts and getting the word out as best I can, but still people have been reluctant to seize the opportunity to be part of something special, no matter how charismatic I sound on the airwaves. Those who get in touch want to know how much exposure they'll receive and what return they'll get on their investment. For them, an epic feat of endurance is little besides a numbers game where winning means turning a profit.

When Adam strolls through the pub wearing a colourful shirt, schooner in hand, I immediately have a feeling that he's someone who'll get behind me. We chat about the history of his brand and about my crazy plan. After half an hour of this, Adam turns to James.

'How much do you guys need?'

James gives him the run-down, talks about fuel, food, gear, travel costs. He talks about my mission to make an impact and partnership with We Are Mobilise. He tells Adam about the record I'm hoping to break.

Adam listens, nods approvingly now and then. When James invites questions, Adam has just one.

'How's ten grand sound?'

Our first sponsorship is locked down.

It's a gamble on Adam's part. Not once in this meeting does he question anything – be it my athletic ability or the feasibility of the run. He's seen what I achieved with the fifty marathons and the 200 laps of Bronte hill and wants in on whatever I'm doing next. He's spent his adult life chasing after things that ignite his passion. For a businessman, he's not too fussed about monetary success. He simply wants to get behind those things that excite him and those people that can make a difference.

Two weeks later, I'm sitting on the couch of Channel 9's *Today* show in a pair of Budgy Smugglers, telling a live audience about my upcoming run. Afterwards, I meet with Puma, who see a well-meaning kid who wants to change the world. Rather than ask for a guaranteed return on any investment, they instead take a leap, agreeing to dedicate a significant portion of their marketing budget to helping this thing of mine come to life. And they may have just saved the day: without Puma's Daniel 'Pancho' Gutstein and Neysa Goh, 'Nedd's Record Run' wouldn't be getting off the ground.

Slowly but surely, as more people get involved and donations start coming in, the pipedream begins turning into a reality, and I feel the pressure lift from my shoulders. My priority now is to ensure my body gets to the starting line not only in one piece but finely tuned. I need a running coach.

24

Belly knows a coach by the name of Matty Abel and suggests I give him a call. I wonder how I might put things. What's the best way to tell someone you've never met that you want to run across Australia, averaging 100 kilometres a day? How do you articulate it in such a way that the next thing you hear isn't the sound of the other guy disconnecting?

While I do my best to sound rational, Matty seems unconvinced.

'Riiiiiight,' he says, his voice thick with scepticism. I hear a sharp exhale of breath, which I assume to have occurred concurrently with a rolling of the eyes.

Oh, this fucking dickhead, he was likely thinking. And I don't blame him.

But if Matty harbours doubts, he doesn't voice them in my earshot. Instead, he gets to work creating a training program that specifies exactly how far and how often I'm going to run, along with details of the complementary strength training I'd do around it.

Naturally, I follow his blueprint to the best of my ability – but that's not saying much, unfortunately.

I try. So hard. But I just can't. Where Matty wants an eight-kilometre run in the morning, I do twelve. Where he prescribes twelve kilometres in the evening, I run seventeen after work.

I don't tell him the real distances I'm amassing. Instead, I just go out, stop my watch when I hit his quota and let that upload, then continue on my merry way without logging the extra kays. Does he know what I'm up to? Probably. I think we have a tacit understanding. I think he knows exactly how my mind works. *Sorry, coach, I always have to go that little bit further. I always have to do more.* So, Matty is trying to tame the beast, prescribing fewer kilometres than he knows I'll do, but figuring the numbers he gives me will limit my excesses to some extent.

On the weekends, if I have a fifty-kilometre run on the program, Matty likely knows I'll do sixty. It might sound like his expertise is wasted on me, but while I deviate from his instructions on volume, I certainly treat them as a guide, and I appreciate the structure he's putting in my days. I'd needed someone I trusted to tell me what to do and to break down my training into morning and evening blocks. Via Training-Peaks, an online platform that syncs data from my GPS across each workout, Matty can analyse my performance and see if, and on what days, I'm overtraining, and then come up with ways to reel me in. The guy's a problem-solver. He finds alternative ways for me to push myself when injury seems imminent, plonking me on a bike or pointing me towards a pool but never suggesting I put my feet up because he knows he'd be wasting his breath.

Belly knew something about Matty before I did: here's a coach with heaps of clients to his name who understands the importance of catering to the individual rather than brandishing some blanket program that might work wonders for you but maim someone else. He's able to sit back and go, *'Okay, this person's well-conditioned with a mind like this – he should do this . . .'* He's coached runners for multi-day ultra-endurance events and ultra-marathons in mountainous regions, and completed many of these runs himself. But until now he'd never coached someone to run across Australia, never had to wrangle a personality so prone to redlining his capabilities.

He wants me on the start line injury free. How to do it is the hard part. He has no precedent to invoke, certainly not when the runner is a twenty-three-year-old who's still relatively new to the sport. And yet, Matty never seems to doubt his ability to do the job. I've known from our first conversation that he's a guy I want in my corner.

With Matty's guidance, my running is back to a point where I'm feeling more excited than agitated at the prospect of another physical challenge. But just as my kilometre count is rising and all I want is to be out there on the Nullarbor, the pain in my tibia returns – only this time it's worse, like an ice-pick being driven into my shin at each torturous step.

I don't admit it to Matty or James, but I'm scared. The start date for the run has been set for 1 September 2022. It is now May, and the months ahead will be critical in terms of preparing my body for what's to come. As for how you prepare *mentally* for 100 kilometres a day when your body can't cope with 100 kilometres in a week, well, that, for now, is beyond me.

To admit to the pain would be to open myself up to criticism and doubt from sponsors and pundits alike. Even without this setback, a cloud of uncertainty hovers over the operation. In conversations I'm having, people's incredulity is palpable. Yes, we're landing sponsors. But their willingness to stick will be tested by any revelation of injury – and besides, I can't bear the thought of letting anyone down. I've asked them to take a leap of faith and they have, and they don't need to hear I'm in a bit of strife and start regretting ever hearing my name. I want them to be able to celebrate their act of risk-taking, their plunge into the unknown. I want them to come to think of it as the best decision they'd ever made.

25

Running becomes unbearable. I'm convinced it's a bone injury and my running days are numbered. At the end of May, I return to the farm and confide in Mum, spill my doubts and fears about the run and my sponsors.

Together, we make the 120-kilometre drive from Forbes to Orange for an MRI, then stop at a cafe on the return journey to await the results. Stress has ruined my appetite, so I sit, blankly stirring my coffee.

'What if you pushed it back, even if just a little bit?' suggests Mum. 'Could you do it in April next year?'

I look up at her. 'Absolutely not. I'm not waiting another six months to get it done. I can't, Mum.'

The months of training I'm staring down will be critical, but at the same time I know that no amount of training will adequately prepare me for the run, and therefore these feelings of uncertainty I'm battling are something I need to accept. Were I to push back the start date because of injury, then it would be easy down the track to push it back again due to lack of fitness or some variable outside of my control. Ultimately, I have to trust that my mind is up to the challenge, and that while my body is going to protest violently at numerous points along the way, it will be my mind that carries me to success. I will never truly be ready, but I will have to start regardless.

I call James ahead of getting the MRI news.

'Look, mate, I'll tell you the results when I get them, but just trust me that we'll get there,' I say.

I figure I'll be setting off on the scheduled date, and that whatever happens, happens; that I'll die by the sword with my head held high. People have gotten behind me and I will not let them down. I will push on. Move forward. It's the only direction I can accept.

The results come back: what I'm feeling is a stress response, not a bone injury.

It's go time.

26

In the countdown to launch, each week feels like a month. Time ticks by slowly, and every day that I set off to my job site in my hi-vis vest and boots reminds me of what I'm *not* doing: living each day with passion, pursuing a higher purpose, challenging myself to be better. I know that after this run is done, no matter how it all plays out, I won't be coming back to this life as an electrician. How do I put this? I need to live life on a ledge that few have ever dared to walk along, where survival depends on feel and gut instinct, agility and quick thinking.

Every morning I rise predawn and lace up my trainers. I stand outside in the stillness that prevails before even the garbage trucks have begun roaring along the streets. I feel forever alone. It's my will that keeps driving me forward – and the knowledge that soon the training will be done, and I'll be running for real on some endless stretch of outback bitumen, dodging road trains and road kill, breathing heavily, carried by legs that feel busted and broken. And right now, all I want is to be in the thick of it. I know there'll be times when the pain will seem too much to bear, but surrounding those moments will be an intoxicating sense of adventure. This is an opportunity a precious few will ever have, and fewer still will see through to the end.

IT'S THE LAST WEEK of August when the plane lands in Perth and I shuffle down the aisle to the metal stairs that lead to the tarmac. Unlike the other passengers, I have a spring in my step that may or not be noticeable to those milling around the arrival gate. Do they assume the grin on my face belongs to someone who's about to be reunited with a loved one, or is there something about it that speaks to the thrill of heading into battle?

I arrive on my own and expect to feel some sense of unease around managing in a city I don't know, but it's not there. Instead, I feel switched on, eager to start my journey. In seven days, I'll be in unfamiliar territory: new pains, new challenges, new conflicts that rage internally and threaten to put this enterprise on its knees. I step out of the airport into the sunshine, welcoming every thought and sensation.

I could have started the run in Sydney, but if there's one thing I know, it's that my mind and body will be cooked upon completion of this journey. And the last thing I want is to finish and then, hours later or the next day, be lying prostrate in an airport terminal, waiting for a flight home. I figure that with friends and some family in Sydney, it'll make for a special finish if the endpoint is Bondi Beach – as long as they can be bothered to come out and see me stagger home.

The Airbnb I'm staying in is a heritage-listed house in Fremantle with high ceilings and spacious rooms. With its creaky timber flooring and sandstone walls, it's the kind of place you know carries at least a century of history, its ghost stories as obvious as its dust.

I'll be spending a few nights here alone before my crew arrives. It feels like the place is trying to tell me something: *What the hell are you getting yourself into?* With its dark hallways and period features, I walk into rooms and have the uneasy feeling that someone's crawling underneath the floorboards.

On a morning coffee run a few days after arriving, I sense eyes upon me, like those of the barista who cocks an eyebrow as he takes in the mullet and uniform of running shoes and sweat-wicking shorts.

'I hadn't seen you before and you've been coming to this shop for the last three mornings,' he says. 'What brings you here?'

'I'm running across Australia,' I say. 'Running from Cottesloe Beach to Bondi Beach in forty-three days. Come out September 1 and send us off.'

There's a laugh, a shake of the head, then silence. Perhaps I wouldn't believe me either if I were in his shoes. But it's all too real for me now. The air feels laced with freedom. The future is an object to be moulded. Everything is possible.

At times like this, normal life becomes a waiting room. Seated, you watch as the minutes crawl by, collecting with a thud at the bottom of the hourglass while still your name has not been called. I have a routine, though, to keep me sane: I rise with the sun, then brave an ocean dip that coats my skin in goosebumps. I stay off my feet as much as I can, trying to push the knee pain that won't go away to the most distant corners of my mind. I talk to locals, learn their names and their stories, breakfast at a leisurely pace at the start of days that are largely free of obligations. It's all so comfortable – and that scares me a touch. I don't want to get used to this, a quiet life of simple pleasures.

One morning, a newly made friend, Ian Smith, greets me just as the sun is bleeding out into the skyline, casting orange embers into the sea. I've seen Ian every morning in the changing rooms of the North Cottesloe SLSC, which is where I rinse the salt off my body after my dip. On the first morning, I looked to my left and saw the hairless arse of an elderly man. By the third day, I figured I should really put a face to the backside, so I reached out in greeting. Instantly, I saw in his countenance ample evidence of a life well-lived. Even in his eighties, there was something childlike about him – the kind of alert, wonder-filled inquisitiveness that normally fades with age and accrued disappointments. Now on the beach, Ian's eyes take in my shivering body.

'Are you going to come up for a coffee?' he asks.

Over breakfast, Ian asks what I'm doing alone in Perth. I tell him about the run and see my own enthusiasm reflected in his wide-eyed gaze. His lips curl into a smile that reaches his crinkled eyelids. 'You're running!' he practically yells across the table.

Ian has disturbed the peace. Club regulars, who appreciate their quiet mornings spent poring over newspapers against the backdrop of hushed conversation and the whirr of milk thickening into a delicate froth, now find themselves pulled into this unusual conversation. Ian talks about my run with the reverence of a pastor delivering an Easter sermon; just hearing of it has been enough to turn him into a believer.

The good word spreads. I walk into cafes and have baristas asking about my starting point, vowing to get as many people as they can down there on the Thursday morning. When I walk into a pub at dinnertime, I feel an energy shift, an excitement that seems to coat the walls like thick paint, its fumes intoxicating all around.

So unexpected, their support overwhelms me. I'm more used to having to convert the negativity of naysayers into fuel, but it feels like everyone here on the other side of the country wants to see me succeed. Maybe they have this idea of me – accurate – as someone who shows up every day with little besides an unbreakable determination to get the job done. And maybe in me they can see a part of themselves, or at least would like to: approaching whatever challenge they may face in the same spirit, sensing or knowing that to succeed you don't need a particular genetic makeup or a childhood spent learning the intricacies of whatever it is you're pursuing. You just need to get cracking and follow through.

27

They're standing outside the airport terminal when I pull up in the team van that Mum's named Bertha: Jemma, Dad, Bradley, James and our videographer, Sam. Some might think it's a lousy idea to have friends and family as your crew on a colossal run: too emotional; too many feelings and sensitivities for me to consider at the expense of a single-minded focus on the task. But I wouldn't have it any other way.

I'd met Bradley at a recovery centre in Sydney's Surry Hills. I was in the thick of my 50-in-50 when I glanced at this guy who had a pea-soup Yorkshire accent sitting next to me with his legs jammed into a pair of compression boots. Weeks later, we bumped into each other on a run from Bondi to Manly, and on the ferry ride home struck up a conversation about all things running and life. Chatting with Bradley, I sensed that what we had was more than a shared interest in running; we were more like brothers in suffering – both of us longed for the kind of tests of endurance and uncharted paths that would strike fear into ordinary folk.

Jem I'd met on the third-last day of my 50-in-50. She'd arrived at Centennial Park with the sister of a mutual friend, and the moment I saw her, I knew she was someone I wanted to get to know. Unfortunately, I didn't make a smooth start of things. Though she'd introduced herself to me, for some reason I called her Georgia (in my defence, forty-eight marathons in a row will turn your brain to mush). Thankfully, she looked past that slip-up and kept up with me, lap after lap around Centennial Park, eventually running what to that point was her personal-best distance of thirty-two kilometres. That evening, unable to get the chocolate eyes and cheeky smile of this woman out of my mind, I went through the unread messages clogging up my Instagram and saw she'd reached out. Three days later, I met her at Clovelly beach with the hope of soaking up both the sun and her company. The rest, as they say, is history.

It was through James I met Sam, who worked as a videographer for Bursty. From the start, he was warm, though I also sensed he had his guard up a bit. Sam speaks softly and sparingly, but when he does speak, you listen. Gradually, his walls came down and this gentle bloke from Torquay, Victoria, with a fertile mind became a dear friend.

Reunited, we're like kids swarming outside the canteen for a lunchtime special, talking over one another and unable to play it cool as others look on wondering what all the fuss is about.

There's still so much to organise over the final two days: food to be bought, a trailer to be kitted out, logistics to be nailed to ensure safety and efficient communication out on the road. Somehow, we need to get a van from the east coast to the west coast, a task that would have been a nightmare had I not received a direct message from Michael Rugendyke at Team Global Express, offering to help.

As Michael put it, 'I can get anything to anywhere in the country, within one-and-a-half days.'

Thank God for people like Michael.

With his help, we're able to add to our fleet of vehicles a ute fixed with a teardrop trailer (Jemma will drive that), along with a campervan for Mum and Dad.

I'm touched by the presence of those around me and the help I'm receiving. I take neither for granted. Mum and Dad were always going to cross the country for me, but the others? It's their time they're giving up and their time they won't get back. I might be running alone, but their role in getting me to the finish line will be nothing short of crucial.

The only problem is, none of us has much of an idea what to do at this point, something that becomes abundantly clear when we stroll into the Highgate Woolworths armed with a grocery list that is patently inadequate.

What does one eat when trying to run 100 kilometres a day? What do you stock up on to sustain that kind of mileage and kickstart your recovery night after night? There's probably a far more scientific approach we could follow if we knew any better, but in my mind the two staples are sugar and carbohydrates. I march through the aisles with Jem and Bradley, our trolley's wheels barely rolling under the weight of items piled high. We throw in packets of bread rolls and boxes of muesli bars and Weet-Bix. There's enough honey and biscuits in there to feed an army, along with a kilogram each of bacon, cheese and beef jerky.

The odd shopper casts a disapproving look over the contents of the trolley, mystified as to what our choices suggest about our lifestyle. I want to think we have it all under control. But watching Jem and Brad throw in bottles of Gatorade, huge blocks of KitKat and umpteen tubs of two-minute noodles makes me realise we are not a well-oiled machine. No. This is a bloody crapshoot in which each of us is just making our best guess at things.

We have no idea about where we'll happen upon our first food outlet to top up supplies, or when we might have access to fresh fruit and vegetables. It's like going camping without knowing how long you'll be gone or how much you need to pack to satiate everyone's hunger.

The frenzy continues right up to the night before. I'm practically jumping out of my skin with excitement. The desire I feel to be out there running is becoming impossible to suppress, and all I can do is be thankful that the final countdown is on. By tomorrow, I will be on my long and agonising way to Sydney. And I won't miss my Fremantle digs. I hadn't realised just how terrifying they were until the arrival of the crew, whose expressions of unease bordering on terror confirmed this place would make a great setting for a horror flick. None of us wants to be left alone anywhere in the house. We decide to hunker down as a group in the living room, with its large, musty armchairs. Safety in numbers, if you like.

For our final dinner we pile ready-made lasagne into our mouths as James, who's liaised with various state roads authorities, gives me a rundown on logistics.

'Right mate, you're going to have to wear hi-vis every day,' he says. 'And you can't run before sunup or after sundown.'

Incredulous, I stare at him. I'm setting out to break a record. I'm prepared to submit my body to hell to ensure I keep ahead of schedule by running 100 kilometres a day. I've set certain rules for myself, such as I can't stop until five

My on-road team minus Jem who is taking the photo. *From left:* Belly, myself, James (Uncle Jimmy), Sammy Dennis, Dad, Mum and Bradley. We are all tucking into a feed at the Balladonia roadhouse. I was in a lot of pain this night.

Day 3 of the run. Just when I thought the wind and the hills couldn't get any worse, road trains and rain started to come thick and fast.

I was so cold even my fingers started to freeze up. We didn't have gloves so I opted for a pair of Posisocks to keep my hands warm, but they didn't help at all.

The end of day 3. Starting to feel the freedom of deliberate insanity.

I was so excited when we hit the 90 mile straight. It was something I had been thinking about for a long time. Note the strapping tape on my shin. This was about the time things started to fall apart.

Some days were just rolling hill after rolling hill. Every time I got to the top of one, my heart sank as I saw another.

We were so lucky to see Australia in all its glory, one step at a time.

We were blessed with some picturesque sunrises. Almost every morning I was running into the sunrise and I got used to the sun setting on my back.

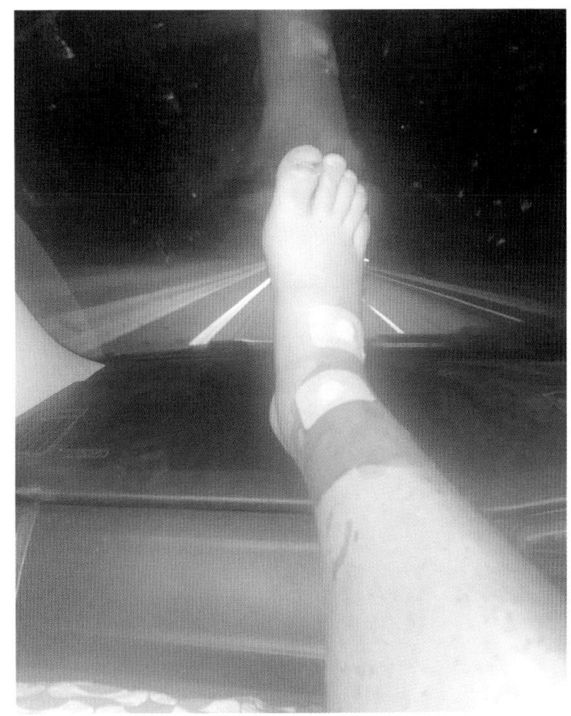

This is my ankle post-injection driving back across the Nullarbor to where we finished day 13. I was completely oblivious to the pain I was about to put myself through.

Note the flies on my head. I think even they wanted me to stop. This was the first day post-injection. I ran 100 kilometres that day and 675 kilometres that week. Despite the pain I was in, I felt completely unstoppable.

It was special to have the whole family together for a few days out on the run. Memories for a lifetime.

This was the windiest day on the Nullarbor. We had 50 km/h headwinds and the only reprieve was to run behind Bertha for seven hours. That was pure torture.

The road trains kept on coming.

Mum knows me best. I was not well this day, but as usual, we found a way forward. Nothing like an honest meat pie to warm the soul.

I was 95 kilometres into this day. We arrived at Port Augusta still in daylight to a spa bath and a king-size bed. What a day.

in the evening, even if I manage to clock 100 kilometres for the day before then. I'm treating this like a job, determined to bring the utmost commitment and professionalism to the task. It's like James has no idea what makes me tick, what I'm capable of or what I'm willing to subject myself to. He must sense something now, though, if only the rage burning behind my eyes.

'I'm not breaking this record unless I'm running three hours before sunrise and for three hours after sunrise,' I tell him.

On this issue, James and I agree to disagree. But come the night, lying in bed, I know I won't be waiting for tomorrow's sunrise to be my starting gun. I hardly sleep at all. It isn't nervousness that keeps me awake, so much as excitement and a fear of the unknown. I can put together 100-kilometre efforts back-to-back. That I know. And my mind will do all it can to ensure I keep showing up, day after day until the run is done. But I also know my knees will swell up so badly that I'll need litres of anti-inflammatory gel just to keep the pain at bay. And my hips and other joints and muscles essential to running will soon follow in screaming their protestations. It's all just a matter of time.

And I don't want to wait a minute longer.

I sit awake at three in the morning, the sky still black. My phone glows in my hand, good-luck messages pouring in from family and friends. I decide not to open Instagram. Enough already. It's all just noise now. After what feels like years of waiting, the day has arrived and all I can think of is how much I've wanted this – a challenge of this magnitude, a challenge that has shaped my life and given it meaning.

The crew emerges from their beds, and where you might expect to see tiredness creasing their faces, all you see are the wild eyes of fellow thrill seekers. My stomach is churning but not from hunger. I force down a bacon-and-egg roll, taking pains to chew each mouthful thoroughly to minimise the risk of anything coming up again on the run. Brad, Jem, Sam and Dad climb into the back of the van as I take my seat behind the wheel. I turn around briefly to flash them a smile, then I crank the volume on Norman Greenbaum's *Spirit in the Sky* as we make our way down to Cottesloe Beach.

As the van edges closer to the start line, I see movement along the promenade. Some forty people have gathered, most of them strangers to me. They're braving the morning chill to be part of this adventure, and I absorb the cheers that sound from faces obscured by the hoodies of fleece-lined jackets.

This is it. This is Cottesloe, the start of it all. There's a news camera in place, and presenter ready to do a live-cross back to the studio. But I've got a run to prepare for and flick the media duties to Jemma.

Without so much as a quick jog on the spot or a set of star jumps, without fanfare of any sort, I'm off, legs turning over in quick strides under a sky still bruised by twilight, a smile stretched across my face. I'm thinking of nothing besides the 100 kilometres that lie ahead on roads I've yet to explore. On the phone I'm clutching, I fire up Google Maps and try to work out where the fuck I have to go.

28

DAY 1. COTTESLOE BEACH, PERTH

I can see Dad in Bertha parked off the side of the road, where he's holding a sign urging drivers to slow down and exercise caution – all for the benefit of my lone figure, loping along in monotonous strides. From rolled-down, passenger-side windows, heads pop out to yell words of encouragement that are lost on the wind. Some drivers stop when they reach Dad, grabbing wallets and foraging in handbags for cash to donate to the cause of homelessness. It's all happening now, and I can feel my spirits soaring, as though I'm bursting with an energy that could carry me all the way home.

I can't see the ute carrying Jemma and Brad, though. The streets are still too narrow, too suburban for the crew to cruise alongside me.

I try to steady my fingers as I fire off a text to Jemma.

Meet me at the BP station. 25 km out from the start.

The kilometres tick by, effortlessly enough. It's not that I'm feeling no pain, but the pain is finally achieving something. I'm aware of the patellofemoral discomfort – it won't be going away any time soon. I stupidly didn't tape my nipples or oil up my inner thighs before setting out, and I'm feeling the effects of those blunders already. But like I said, it's all manageable. Despite all these aches, pains and stabbing hurts that erupt from various body parts, my mind dances over them, knowing all of this is to be expected.

I think of those months spent working on job sites and the feelings of emptiness that followed me home. I think of how easy it is to sit around waiting for inspiration to strike, or for everything to be just so before you act. I think of the leap of faith I've taken – a faith in the power of my mind and body to finish what I've just started. And so, I run, knowing that I'm no longer waiting for anyone or anything, but creating something for myself. I run knowing that I'm doing the very thing that makes my life worth living.

After fifty kilometres, I stop for food. Jem's trying to make me a toasted sandwich, but our generator's not working and there's no way to toast the bread. She eyes the service station across the road and, without hesitation, unplugs the toaster and tucks it under her arm. She also gathers up the contents of the sandwich and takes off.

She returns minutes later with the toastie, flashing me a smile. The message is clear: okay, we had a minor setback, but nothing we couldn't fix on the fly.

With one hand clutching my sandwich and the other enlarging Google Maps, I try to get my head around the next 50 kays. It's then I see a post from one of my team flash up on my screen.

50 kilometres down, 3950 kilometres to go.

That's the caption beneath a video of me running up a gnarly east Perth hill.

The numbers hit me like a week's worth of bad news. To see them written down like that is to realise suddenly the absurdity of it all. It's like an impossibly long to-do list, so long that it inspires a sense not of an urgency but paralysis.

How do you comprehend it? How do you begin to tackle it?

But I won't allow myself to think this way.

My crew was only trying to show its support and celebrate the erasure of the first 50 kays, but they've misread how I work. My mind works by seeing a massive task not in its entirety but as a series of chunked-up mini assignments to be addressed one at time. The task today is 100 kilometres. That's all I want to think about it. Don't portray it as the first brick laid in the Great Wall of China.

By eighty-two kilometres, I want food because I'm hungry and not just because I need it for fuel. Jem finds a bakery and I allow myself to be carried through its doors on air that smells impossibly sweet. It's as though I can taste the pastry just by running my eyes over the numerous pie varieties, and suddenly all I want is to eat a pie every day for as long as it takes me to reach Sydney.

I bite into one and the warmth of gravy-laden steak coats my throat on its way down, the steam rising from the pie mimicking that coming off my sweat-soaked body.

I keep waiting for the high to pass – this excitement, this adrenaline. But as the kilometres tick by on this the first day, I grow not more tired but more enthusiastic; I can't believe how lucky I am that this will be my life for the next seven weeks.

I don't allow myself to stop at the 100-kilometre mark, despite my body feeling jammed into the upright position to the point where I'm loath to sit down. For one thing, it's only 4:30 in the afternoon. For another, I know that as the days go by and my body becomes stiff as a rod, I will get slower.

The mornings will become harder, and it will take longer for me to reach that flow-state in which everything seems to be working in perfect unison. So, I push on. Just like any other job, there'll be no leaving early. Only when it's 5 pm and I've added a bonus three kilometres onto the daily quota do I allow Jem to mark the ground with pink spray paint, signalling the starting point of tomorrow's run.

Whatever rules James had in my mind as far as road safety are concerned go out the window at this point. Taking in my hunched posture and the pained expression on my pale face, he finally understands the depths I'm prepared to go to in order to break the record.

'Do what you need to do,' he says.

I hadn't allowed myself to think about it, but as soon as I stop the GPS, fatigue hits me like a landslide. Nothing feels stable underfoot and each step brings a jolt of pain so acute that it takes all my mental strength to shift my attention onto something else.

I'd imagined finishing and getting straight into an ice bath, followed by a hot shower that washes away all trace of the day's suffering. But the reality is a different story, one that feels like a fever-dream. There's a flurry of movement around me, panic as the crew realises nothing has been set up. No one's even bought the ice to dump into the bath that Dad is struggling to blow up as you would an inflatable mattress. A party departs for the nearest service station to get essentials, but a full hour passes and I'm still in dirty running gear, yet to begin the all-important recovery process.

By the time we sit down for dinner, tomorrow's alarm has already been set.

Jem opens the door of the teardrop trailer, inside of which we've managed to squeeze a mattress for me to sleep on and a doona for warmth. It's a basic sleeping arrangement, but when you've just run 100 kilometres, you're less concerned with life's comforts than you are with simply getting horizontal and hoping sleep descends swiftly. I feel as if the day's effort has excavated my soul, leaving nothing in its wake. I left it all out there on Perth's long and winding roads. And just when I want to slip into unconsciousness, all I can feel is pain. No position is comfortable and rolling and turning in an effort to find one that might be is torture. So, I simply lie still, thinking of the days to come, while the heat coming off my body turns the trailer into a sauna. Because there's no ventilation, fat droplets of condensation begin to rain down from the roof, soaking the doona. *Oh shit*, I think. *I'm in for it.*

There'll be no sleeping tonight.

29

DAY 2. NORTHAM CARAVAN PARK, WESTERN AUSTRALIA

Once, during training, I had run 100 kilometres and woken the next morning to go again (even though, at that point, Matty had prescribed just a six-kilometre follow-up effort). It was excruciating. If you've run a marathon, you know the stiff-legged stagger that you're reduced to using the next day. Your calves feel like they've taken bullets while your hips practically rotate your entire trunk with each lift of the leg. You walk with all the ease and grace of a toddler, though minus their glorious and joyful confidence.

Waking up on day two brings a pain worse than I felt after that 100-kilometre training run. And this time, there'll be no leisurely six-kilometre jog with which to ease my body into active recovery. I tell myself that I just need to get moving and trust that my body will sort itself out, that these overwhelming feelings of stiffness will fall away with each passing minute as I run.

I set off at 4:30 am, knowing minutes will be lost as I grope for some degree of rhythm amid the pain. For ten kilometres, I can only shuffle, the light from my headtorch bouncing off the road. The headwinds spring up immediately, lashing at me, piercing my layers and chilling bone. In the quiet, I hear each strained breath.

If yesterday felt easy, today is the opposite. Everything requires intense effort. Simply putting one foot in front of the other constitutes an act of defiance. I feel like I'm stuck in a wind tunnel and running in slow motion, arms pumping and knees driving for hours on end for paltry progress. I glance at the GPS and promise myself not to look at it again for a long time. When I do, it feels like a decade has passed. Everything has slowed down, me especially. When, at last, I finish, I don't want to talk to anybody. I just want to climb into the teardrop trailer and tell myself that the hardest day is behind me, that I'll never experience worse.

As soon as those familiar pellets of water start landing heavily on my face and limbs, I almost laugh. What wishful thinking! Of course, things can and will get worse.

The trailer rattles in the unrelenting wind as rain cuts diagonally through the air. By the time my alarm goes off at 3:30 am, nothing can be salvaged from the storm. I've been lying here awake all night, listening to the rain and shivering in my own sweat, knowing further discomfort is inevitable because there'll be no blue sky today.

Crouched alone in Bertha, I pour hot water from the kettle over six Weet-Bix, then drown them in the powdery taste of long-life milk and enough honey to send you reeling from a sudden assault of sugar. It's a soggy mush I shovel into my mouth with a sense of disgust. Fuelled up, I shove my wrinkled feet into shoes and step out onto the Great Eastern Highway, its surface slick and slippery from rainfall. *One of them fucking days, hey.*

At once, yesterday's headwinds seem like nothing. Today, they're just as strong but mixed with rain, and the combination seems to cut through my skin, leaving me feeling raw and exposed.

At the first rest stop, I can barely make eye contact with Jem, Brad or Sam, and the mood is as sombre as the weather forecast. The lively excitement of day one feels like a lifetime ago. Operating on no sleep, I lack the energy to show my crew the appreciation they deserve. To Jemma, who's been shouldering so much – cooking, cleaning, navigating, sorting out my recovery and hydration needs and copping torrents of abuse from truckies out on the road – I can't offer affection. To do so would be too dangerous, because in her reciprocal affection would lie the ultimate comfort; emotionally and mentally, it would choke me up and break me down.

I wear my discomfort like an impenetrable armour. Me, the crew, we're all in deep. If they didn't know what they were getting themselves into before we started, they can see it now. My eyes, feral and ferocious, are fixed on something in the distance, and it's calling me forward. I'm like a wounded dog that's been beaten into a corner, untrusting of anyone that extends a hand in support. To survive, I have to attack. My breath disperses before my eyes like smoke and when I scream, I scream to no one as I channel every ounce of pain into fuel. I asked for this. For months it was all I craved. So, onwards: it's the only option.

I'm shaking with cold by the time I get to the ninety-kilometre mark, a full hour behind schedule. As the sun dips ever lower on the horizon, I need to get the headtorch on, a tangible reminder of the hours I'm losing from recovery. I shouldn't still be out here. My body seems to have lost its ability to generate heat and I feel like a tent that's deflating. Lips blue. Ears frozen. A nose that won't stop running. Jem tentatively hands me a pie – the glimmer of hope I've hung onto all day – but even flaked pastry and meat does little to lift my spirits. She turns to me, fixes me with those wide eyes that seem to convey truth.

'I've never seen anything like it, Nedd.'

The words pull me back to the moment. Right now, I'm on the edge of something – a struggle unlike any I've known before or could have imagined. I lack the words to describe it and even a barrage of expletives wouldn't help. But words might be superfluous, anyway. The anguish is written on my face, which is worn and crumpled like a used napkin.

But there'll be no throwing in the towel. With ninety kilometres down, I've got just ten more to knock off before I can say I've made it through this day from hell. If I want to find out what I'm truly capable of, it's moments like these that will deliver the answers.

I don't say anything to Jemma. But as I hit 'resume' on the GPS, it's her words I think of, turning them over in my mind for the remainder of today's run. When I finish, I pull up Strava on my phone and type from the heart.

Come at me WA storms. I am the motherfucking storm.

30

DAY 3. KELLERBERRIN, WESTERN AUSTRALIA

Come the night, every part of me is throbbing, bloodied or rubbed raw. No longer my body's way of signalling stress, pain is now the state I exist in. I have gone past sleep deprivation to nestle up against insanity.

On my mattress, I drift off and suddenly I'm back on the road, being dragged back by fierce headwinds that force me to run the 100 kays all over again. My own screaming jolts me awake and now I fear sleep for the dreams that may come.

I sit up and listen to the percussive rhythm of rain on the trailer's roof, wondering if I'll ever know what it is to feel warm again. The door opens and a familiar face appears. Mum, who arrived with Belly earlier in the evening, stands before me with a smile that dazzles like a camera flash.

'Hey darling,' she says. 'You are the motherfucking storm.'

The pressure valve releases, and I relax. The tears come as forcefully as the rain, steady and insistent, leaving Mum's jacket wet where I've been resting my head. I want to tell her about the pain, have her examine my knees and ankles and see the swelling that has made my shoes feel three sizes too small. I want to tell her about the blunders made along the way, of evenings spent shivering in wet clothes while watching Dad inflate the ice bath, the rest of the crew scrambling in the darkness to sort out dinner and sleeping arrangements. I want to warn her of the person I'm becoming out here on the road, someone so far removed from comfort that I don't know how to relate to anyone anymore. I want to tell her about the team and all they've shouldered in the last three days, solely for my benefit. I want to tell her that the risk of burnout is real and rising.

But with Mum, words are superfluous. In normal times, she can gauge my mood just by the way I greet her and knows how I'm feeling even with my back turned. She can read me better than anyone I know. And her presence casts a certain calm that hangs in the air like pollen, before falling on those around her.

I need her here. The crew does, too. Everyone is spent, exhausted from the long days and rough nights and my taking out my frustrations on each of them. Spot fires surround us. Another day without her and we'd have imploded, the central task buried under our internal struggles.

Mum immediately extinguishes the flames. She speaks to Brad and Sam, lends an ear to Dad, and brings comfort to Jem, who has felt so alone in her be-on-top-of-everything role. It's been a mess, each of us focused solely on getting from one point to the next with little regard for efficiency or the power of routine. With Mum here, it feels like order has been restored.

I knew this would be hard – I'm not a fool – but the last two days have tested me beyond what I'd thought possible, especially so early in the run. Still, I've shown up. Each day,

I've got the job done. I don't want to be comfortable, don't want to reveal a soft underbelly, but I do need to feel and draw on the strength of every person around me. Everyone is important but Mum is the light around which we all crowd. Having seen her, having released the negativity that was building up inside me, a flicker of warmth returns to my body, enough for me to close my eyes and know there's nothing tomorrow can throw at me that I won't be able to overcome.

31

DAY 11. SOMEWHERE BETWEEN BALLADONIA AND CAIGUNA, WESTERN AUSTRALIA

This morning, I know something is off.

Yesterday, I'd started coming apart. The run had ceased to be a fun or stirring adventure. Every minute required a conscious effort to grit my teeth and push on.

Those niggles and aches that had been troubling me from the outset are still there, only now they've been eclipsed by the sort of pain that jolts you alert like a newborn's scream in the night. It's my body's last-ditch effort to send a signal to my brain: *Danger imminent!* Except I ignore it.

I thought my body would have adapted by now. I'd been so sure that, after seven days, it would be operating like a machine. I hadn't been naïve enough to think that it wouldn't be hurting from the accumulated stress and laughably inadequate recovery, but I hadn't expected it to be *this* bad. I hadn't expected that I'd still be struggling to sleep at night, or that the inflammation that turns my body into a furnace wouldn't have settled, or that it would take me hours each day to find a little running rhythm, or that for ten kilometres or more

I'd be capable only of shuffling along, willing myself not to stumble into the path of a passing road train.

My body has the rigidity of someone hit by a taser, everything stretched taut, deformed by cramps and exhaustion. I put all my faith in Belly to coax muscles back from a state of alarm into semi-relaxation. Each night I lie down on his treatment table, watch as he casts an evaluative eye over my hips, knees and ankles. He massages aching muscles, tries to do it in a way that won't make me scream, and performs acupuncture on my hips. He ices my ankles to reduce the inflammation and thinks up ways to maximise my recovery, in the process throwing out his physiotherapy training, which would be telling him to order me off my feet until the summer.

Belly's very presence is soothing. He'd lost his dad a week before all this started and I'd all but assumed I'd need to find another physio. But the thing you need to understand about Belly is that he's a guy who invariably shows up for those around him, and here he is doing it for me. Despite all the compassion I felt for him in the circumstances, he was quick to deflect it. He wanted me to focus on the run and just let him be there for me, both as a friend and a physio.

But forty-three days is a long time to be running across the country – and even longer for the support players putting their lives on hold to devote each waking hour to getting me to the finish. After yesterday's 100 kilometres, Belly left, needing to get back to his physiotherapy practice in Sydney and meet pressing family commitments. Though we understood he had to go, we feel his absence keenly.

This morning, I need the guy. I sit awake, readying myself for another day of suffering and aware of an agonising pain in my shin. My ankles – once the stuff of schoolyard taunts for their striking skinniness – are the same size as my calves, two tree trunks attached to the kneecaps. Sleep hovers over me like a fine mist, such that it takes a concentrated effort to stay upright. My movements are slow, my body's actions two steps behind my mind's commands. But I need to get started.

By the time I've covered forty kilometres, I'm running almost two hours behind schedule. As this journey's progressed, I've come to find comfort in routine. These time markers might come to mean little, but right now they're the few things I can control.

If my tank is empty, I rise earlier, knowing I'll need longer to complete the first forty kays by mid-morning. But it's already past noon and I know I need a full hour to rest and eat before I can begin to tackle the next sixty. The day is getting away from me and the stress of it all catches in my shallow breaths. But I'm not done yet. There's still time to salvage a decent result from the day. And so, Jem stands over me, massaging my calves and shins, trying to drive out the fluid that's pressing against bone.

Moving again, I can't find a rhythm. There is no higher gear. Progress comes purely from within, from a realisation that I must bite the bullet and run. As I continue to inch across the Nullarbor along the Eyre Highway, getting ever nearer to the South Australian border, the clock lurches forward and what was to have been a roughly 8 pm arrival is now looking more like 9 pm – hardly ideal when you've got another ten kilometres to cover before you can call it a day. The kitchen at the Cocklebiddy roadhouse, our digs for the night, will call last orders in an hour and I can hear a faint tremble of anxiety in Mum's voice when she phones to tell me this. It's been a tough day for the crew and the longer

I stay out here in failing light, the more dangerous it gets for everyone.

No matter how slow the pace or how painful each stride, it's just another ten kilometres, I tell myself. I'm battle-hardened: every day I've seen 100 kilometres written on the agenda and every day I've knocked them off, no matter the cost. I don't entertain the idea of prematurely calling it a night, if only to snatch some extra recovery before going again tomorrow. I suspect that if I did, something in me would rebel. My body would sense a box unchecked, a to-do list abandoned. Blackness leaks into the sky and the landscape becomes bland and sparse. *Just find a way through*, I tell myself. *Just get it done.*

And I do.

But the wear and tear of eleven days of back-to-back 100-kilometre runs hits me as soon as the GPS ticks over into triple digits. When I reach the roadhouse, I can't even step into the ice bath Dad's prepared for me. My legs protest even the smallest movements, so we compromise: I slide my legs into two plastic bins packed with ice.

There is pain all over my body, but it's the pain in my right shin that my mind won't let go of. Just pressing a fingertip to the bone causes my eyes to roll back in my head. I know this is more than the protests of an angry muscle that's been pushed beyond its limits. This is an injury that threatens to jeopardise the whole shebang.

I think of Belly and the treatments he'd use to get me back out there in the morning. I think of the numerous times he's pulled me back from the brink, stopped a meltdown with some ingenious therapy. I think of everything he's faced in the past few weeks and how he still showed up. Belly would never have let me quit. And neither will I.

32

DAY 12. CAIGUNA, WESTERN AUSTRALIA

I know the situation is dire when I can't even get myself to the toilet during the night. Movement within the coffin-sized bathroom requires a certain nimbleness, and right now I'm taking the kind of laboured steps you'd expect of a wounded elephant. My right foot feels like an anchor attached to my body. I keep trying to lift it, keep trying to put some space between my heel and the floor, but each attempt proves futile. Walking requires stepping with the left, dragging with the right.

Come the predawn, I try to ignore the pain and shove my swollen feet into my running shoes. Maybe it's just a case of the post-run blues, that time of morning when the sky is still black and you're not sure if you're awake or dreaming, where you can still feel the weight of sleep on limbs that weigh heavy with fatigue. My legs are never fully cooperative at this hour. Maybe this is just that and, before I know it, I'll come good.

Wishful thinking. The minutes tick by and the pain doesn't budge. I try to run, and it feels like my shinbone is about to burst through the skin. I want to yell every obscenity under the sun and hear the echo sound across the barren plains, but instead I pull my hoodie down over my head and get to dragging my right foot as I walk on.

I figure that, if this is the state I'm in, then so be it: I'll get to Bondi by walking, even if that means having to walk all day. I begin crunching the numbers: *If I can walk at five kilometres an hour, I'll get the 100 kilometres done in twenty hours. Twenty hours a day – that's it! I'll sleep for a bit at 3 pm and give myself a full hour to eat. But, hey, I can eat and walk at the same time. Then I'll have an hour to shower and freshen up at the end of the day, before another hour or two of shut-eye. And that's the new routine!*

I run it by the crew. They know there's no way I'd be talking crazily about walking to Sydney unless I was physically unable to run, and so the obvious severity of the injury begins to breed concern through the camp. From headwinds that would knock you backwards to the stench of road kill so pungent it could make you puke, my crew has seen me clear every obstacle to date that this challenge has put in front of us. They've seen me slumped defeated at the dinner table, struggling to get food down, only to appear the next morning, shadow-boxing in a roadhouse car park. I'd seemed invincible to them, superhuman, capable of stuff that science couldn't explain. Today, however, I'm as human and vulnerable as the next guy. It's a shock to all of us. But if twenty hours a day of walking is my plan from here on in, they tell me, then consider them onboard.

HOURS PASS AND GETTING my right foot to move, even in a drag, takes all my will. I can feel myself crumbling. I sit down roadside in the fog and put my head in my hands.

I can barely hear my own heavy breathing over the sound of traffic that's just metres from my head. The size and noise of these trucks can be plain terrifying up close. But at this moment, I don't care. If it was road trains I was scared of when starting out, now I welcome them as distractions from near despair.

I see Jemma's ute pull over. She climbs out and tentatively makes her way towards me.

'Just come away from the road, Nedd,' she calls, a hand outstretched, as if she's coming to the aid of a wounded pet.

'I can't run, Jem. I can't run. I've tried and tried and tried.'

She hears the anguish in my voice, knows this guy who won't give up, who always finds a way, is close to cracking. She gets Belly on the phone, and I hear her describing the injury as best she can, with references to severe swelling and crippling pain.

Belly knows how much I want this, how committed I am to reaching Bondi on one leg or two. But he also knows when to draw a line between toughing things out and doing permanent damage to your body. My only hope is that he can see a way for me to keep going without sustaining the latter.

In concert, Belly and Jem put an idea to me. Retire right now for the day or stagger on for a little while longer to notch the marathon distance of a tick over forty-two kays. Get back to the roadhouse. Rest. Fuel up. Get an early night. And trust that all those things combined, especially the extra hours of sleep, will allow my body to fight back and be ready to run again tomorrow.

I'd always said I'd be running 100 kilometres a day. That was the oath I took upon starting this challenge. My crew can see the logic of this new plan and need no convincing, but I'm rattled, and they know it.

'You're still 310 kilometres ahead of the record, Nedd,' says Jemma. 'Just give yourself this little bit of recovery time that will allow you to run on tomorrow.'

It takes everything I have to stop, but when I hit the marathon distance, I switch off the GPS.

It's a case of another day, another test. Each day forces me to relinquish some degree of control. There's a part of me that feels like I've failed, that coming up short today is the result of a mistake I should have been able to avoid. But I also know the intense effort I've sustained since I began this crazy ride. I can taste the salt on my skin and feel sweat caked so thick it could be a layer of clothing. I've lost count of the blood blisters I've developed and the tubes of anti-chafing balm I've emptied.

Sometimes we set out to achieve something and fall short. Sometimes we don't get those things we want. But far from being failures, we are elevated by the act of trying, and carried higher still by our refusal to quit. I still have the fight to keep going. This I know. These times when things don't go as planned, that's when resilience grows. And so I shake off my feelings of disappointment, and choose instead to find courage in the face of adversity.

Back at Cocklebiddy roadhouse, I'm focused solely on recovery – anything that will get me back running as soon as possible. I submerge my right foot in an ice bath for four hours. There's a sense of normality around the dinner table that, paradoxically, feels strange. For starters, it's still light outside. There's been no scrambling to get my sweat-soaked running gear washed and dried in the space of a few hours, nor is anyone having to prop me up in the shower while someone else runs my dinner order over to the kitchen. Time, for once, is on our side – and it's a bloody great feeling, though not one I should get used to.

Despite my doubtful circumstances, there's a lightness to our conversation. We take turns roasting one another, more gentle ribbings over chicken parmis and chips. We share our favourite moments from the trip so far, talk of discoveries made along the way and sights that hang like tapestries in our minds, collectively a vivid portrait of the unseen Australia.

I'm reminded once again how grateful I am to all of them for sacrificing their time for me. I'm grateful for the camaraderie, for their ability to celebrate my wins as their own, and for their preparedness to get in the trenches with me when I'm wounded and low. I look up at Mum, her face creased with fatigue. If I'm bemoaning a lack of sleep, she has it just as rough.

I can't get out of this run until I arrive at Bondi. Finishing is the only option; pain the only certainty. For Mum, my level of commitment has become terrifying. For the first time, she's having to contend with the idea that I may leave it all out here.

33

DAY 13. TWENTY KILOMETRES WEST OF COCKLEBIDDY, WESTERN AUSTRALIA

'I'm just going to fucking walk it,' I tell the crew.

It's 3:30 am and any residual trace of humour from the night before has left my mood. It's back to business – and the plan to walk for twenty hours a day or however long it takes to reach 100 with a leg that won't cooperate. The stars should still be out but any time I direct my gaze upwards, my headtorch obliterates any trace of what might be a beautiful sky.

Sadly, the early bedtime and extra hours' recovery seem to have done nothing for my shin. I awake in agony, which only intensifies with each step towards the starting mark. I'm trying everything I can to get my mind off the pain, but the tears flow anyway. I try to bury myself in the moment, to think only of how each step will bring me closer to today's total, but the prospect of having to continue like this for the remainder of the journey has me seething. My body needs to catch up to my mind! It needs to be just as strong. At very least, it needs to hang in there.

Late morning, I get a call from Belly back in Sydney.

'Nedd, we've got you into Whyalla Hospital tomorrow at 11 am,' he tells me.

Here in Cocklebiddy, it feels like the chances of finding a hospital anywhere close by to run any sort of diagnostics is slim to none. Belly has managed to pull some strings and get me in for scans tomorrow at Whyalla (South Australia), thirteen hours away by car. It's time that I might be able to make up once repaired.

'Mate, they don't generally let people in for two weeks,' says Belly. 'We've managed to get you in. Just take the appointment and go.'

So far today, I've walked only forty kilometres, but the crew senses the urgency in Belly's voice and knows the testing is crucial. As a team, we make the decision for me to go and get scanned.

I turn to Jemma, knowing it's her I want with me on the long drive. She spray-paints my finishing spot for the day, and we head to Madura roadhouse, where Mum, Dad, Sam and Brad are. A short time later, with a chocolate milk in one hand and a soft drink in the other, I head to the ute with Jem, both of us bracing for the long journey ahead.

As I'm walking to the passenger side in my slides, I make a startling realisation. My shin! As if by the flick of a switch, the pain has gone – or almost gone.

My body, starved of easy days and rest for so long, can taste freedom. *This*, it seems to be saying, *this glorious pain-free state, can be yours for the price of just a little extra rest.*

'Jem!' I call out. 'My shin: it's not hurting anymore.'

The expression on Jemma's face says it all. Our wild eyes dart from each other's to the shin that's been plaguing me and back again.

'Try and run on it,' Jem says.

Obediently, I shuffle for fifty metres, kicking up dust with my slides. It's the best I've moved all week. We hop in the ute and turn around, beelining for the mark she'd spray-painted to indicate tomorrow's resumption point.

Are the slides the answer to all my woes? Maybe I can still get the 100 kilometres done. As soon as we find the mark, I'm suddenly hesitant. Belly probably moved heaven and earth to procure me tomorrow's appointment; I can't stick the middle finger up to him now. I fire off a message, alerting him to the success of my fifty-metre slide shuffle.

'My opinion is we should still scan it,' he says. 'There's obviously something going on there. If we can rule out significant bone stress, that's a good thing. If it's severe tenosynovitis, then we can push through that and try to get it to calm down in a short timeframe.'

In other words, time to stop being an idiot and go to Whyalla.

Jem and I climb back into the ute, where it dawns on me that this little detour will put me out of action for fourteen hours, the longest break I've had from running since I started. I know there's something wrong just by looking at the swelling, but I can't help but worry that it might all be psychological. What if I get to the hospital and the scan reveals it's nothing serious, that it's something so minor anyone else could have pushed through? It's only day thirteen and the wheels are coming off. I'd thought that if I had to go to hospital at any point, the decision would be out of my hands. Oh, stuff it. I get in the driver's seat and tell myself to trust Belly.

The drive is long but, around us, Australia comes to life. Running is a great way to see the world. It takes you along stretches you wouldn't otherwise see, lets you be present in a way that driving or commuting or tourist-bus sightseeing would never allow. Each morning, I've seen the day come to life, bathing the landscape in dazzling colour. And each day, I've seen mundane roads turn sublime under the glow of headlights and a soundtrack of thundering trucks. I've marvelled at the beauty as best I can, hindered somewhat by pain and the ever-present need to grind on to meet a brutal schedule.

Now, driving with Jem, I'm undistracted by any need to work out pace, distances or finishing times. We drive and drive, watching the road disappear beneath the windshield as the air blows cold. We look out at bitumen I've yet to run and see infinite possibility. Every reason I felt compelled to take on this challenge is reinforced. Uncertainty might linger around my shin, but all I feel is a determination to resume the run.

34

DAY 14. IN TRANSIT, WESTERN AUSTRALIA

I enter Whyalla Hospital like a tornado.

My legs are two toothpicks dangling from my waist; my toenails, yellow and hardened or missing altogether, are on display in my slides; my face is sunburnt from eyelids to chin. Having not showered properly for days, I'm surely emitting an odour that could kill a weak organism. I'm ragged and strung out, but the need to get this scan done brings a comical animation to my movements.

'Hey, I don't mean to rush anything, but I just want to know timings as I've got a bit of a tight deadline,' I say, trying hard to soften the urgency in my voice with kindness.

But I can tell from the receptionist's pursed lips that I didn't try hard enough. Here she is, working hard, only to have to contend with some guy who's rocked in for a last-minute appointment and has the audacity to act as though he's the one calling the shots. In her shoes, I'd probably be unimpressed, too.

Thirty minutes pass before my name is called and I'm steered towards the MRI machine.

'So, what leg is it?' the radiographer asks.

I point down to my right, then grimace as I raise it.

The radiographer takes in my appearance, her eyes travelling up and down the length of me. I can't work out if she's confused or horrified by what she sees.

'What's, uh . . . what's been happening?' she asks.

'Bit on,' I say. 'Got a big run ahead, so just trying to sort out this injury. Hopefully it's not bone.'

The scan takes twenty minutes. I make my way back to reception, where I ask how long it will take for the results to come through.

'Three days,' she tells me.

Which is two days more than I can afford. The images are instant, of course, but the analysis and report will take time I don't have.

I ask if a rush-order has been placed on my scans – which Belly had told me there would be.

'No,' says the receptionist.

'Sorry,' I say. 'I'm really sorry. But I'm pretty sure there's a rush on this.'

Reluctantly, she takes another look at the referral, and this time sees the rush notification. She looks up at me and smiles.

'I'll see you in an hour,' I say.

Sydney-based sports doctor David Samra calls me an hour later while Jem and I are in the Whyalla Hospital car park. I'm feeling pleasantly full for the first time in weeks, having finally felt comfortable about putting away a reasonably hearty meal – chicken sandwich, scones with whipped cream – knowing it won't be bouncing up and down in my stomach for sixty kilometres.

When I see Dr Samra's name appear on my phone, my stomach drops. As a leading specialist, he has a waiting list that runs long; it can take two months to get an appointment with this guy. To have him on the phone at Belly's request is a privilege. I can only hope he has good news to deliver.

'G'day, mate! How are you going?' Dr Samra says.

He enquires about the run, and I feel my nerves dissipating. My hands are no longer clammy. I get the feeling that the doc has gleaned from Belly that, regardless of the diagnosis, nothing will keep me from that Bondi finish line.

Dr Samra has treated some of the world's best athletes, and there's surprise in his voice as he reviews my scans.

'I can't believe how strong your bones are – it's just incredible,' he says. 'Imagine an old granny: you go in and do surgery on a bone, it's like a knife through butter. With yours, you'd get a diamond drill, and it still wouldn't cut it.'

Great, I've got strong bones. Talk to me, doc!

'So, the good news is your bones are strong. However, you've got an injury.'

Down the line comes a groan, held in the mouth like an extended exhale. I can all but see Dr Samra grimacing at the images, and I shoot Jem a look, expecting the worst.

'Oh, it's a lot of swelling,' he says.

He pauses then before asking me to aim my phone's camera at my leg so he can see it. I comply.

Without even telling me to do anything, he says: 'You can't move it up and down, can you?'

'No.'

'Yep, it's tenosynovitis – the worst tendonitis you can get in a shin before it gets severely infected.'

For any other patient, the prescription would be simple: get your foot in a boot and stay off it for weeks, possibly months, with lots of rehab to follow. But Dr Samra knows not to offer me that shit sandwich.

'Look, I understand the enormity of what's going on, so the other option is, we can try and cortisone it,' he says. 'The thing is, it's not going to get any worse because it's that bad already, but you will be in some of the worst pain you've ever felt.'

It's a trade-off I'm willing to accept if it means being able to run again.

Dr Samra sends a rush on the cortisone injection, and, with Jem, I walk back into the hospital. The stress is leaking out of my pores as I stand at the reception desk, chasing up Dr Samra's referral. I watch the clock, counting the passing minutes. Nothing's come through yet, they tell me. I take a seat in the waiting room, where I make the other patients anxious by my incessant fidgeting.

I give the receptionist a short break from me before going back to the desk to ask her to check again. She finds it!

'Urgent!' she exclaims. 'Jesus, it's urgent, isn't it?'

'Yeah, I'm running across Australia. I need to get back to Cocklebiddy tonight.'

She looks at me, unsure what to make of this information. Before I can explain further, a nurse takes me through to receive the cortisone injection.

In Sydney, cortisone injections into tendons and joints are given all the time. But here in the outback they're a rarity and ordinarily require a notice period of several weeks. By the look on the face of the doctor who greets me, this was not something he was expecting to do today. He raises his eyebrows on reading the referral, then struggles to conceal his nervousness.

'I'm sorry,' he says. 'I don't know what he's trying to get me to do. I don't see why they're telling me to do this. I can't inject your anterior tibialis twice from a lateral point of view. I just don't feel comfortable doing that.'

He looks at me with concern and I feel bad for the bloke. I don't know his background or how often he's given this kind of injection – or if he's ever given it. But we're in this together now.

'Mate, whatever you can put in me, just put it in me,' I tell him with a nod of encouragement.

I can see him mentally preparing himself for the task as he begins rubbing Betadine onto the injection site. He starts talking me through the process and as he counts down from three, Jemma grabs my knee. I feel the liquid being pushed out of the syringe and into my shin. My vision falters and my head jolts back, eyes darting from left to right. I'm acutely aware of the goings-on inside my leg, which feels like a sponge that's soaked up too much liquid and is now expanding and expanding and expanding. Spit bubbles form on my lips as I scream.

Dr Samra was right: it is the worst pain I've ever felt. But the doctor stood up to the task and, in a matter of minutes, the stress of the injection is behind us. He tells me to stay off my feet as much as I can and that I'll need three to four days, *minimum,* before I can return to running. I sneak a glance at Jemma, who stifles a laugh. *No way that's happening,* we're both thinking.

The cortisone won't kick in for another four days, but Dr Samra suggests getting a dictus band, a leather ankle strap fitted with a latex band that I can attach to the laces of my shoe so that each time I pull my hip up while running, the band then pulls my toes towards my knee. Basically, it'll take some pressure off my shin and allow me to plant my foot – so I can go again. I've never heard of such a device, but Jemma sets off for the hospital's orthopaedic ward and miraculously returns holding a dictus band – the last one available, apparently.

Like two fossickers who've struck gold, we can't contain our excitement. The day has been nothing but problem-solving. And while I might have felt disheartened yesterday, our capacity to find solutions to stay in this fight has only hardened my resolve.

I call James as we're walking out of the hospital.

'Just got the injection,' I say. 'Jem and I are on our way back now. Should be there by 5 am.'

He asks if I need to sleep.

'Absolutely not. I'll be running 100 kilometres tomorrow. We're back on.'

I drive five hours west from Whyalla and pull into a service station just outside Ceduna. I pick up a Maxibon and chocolate milk and hand the keys to Jemma.

'Jem, I'm going to hop into the teardrop trailer to sleep and you're going to drive us across the Nullarbor.'

The roads out here aren't exactly a picnic for inexperienced drivers and Jem now has the added pressure of driving a ute with a trailer attached to it through the night as truckies come roaring past with precious little regard for road courtesies. Jem doesn't hesitate, though. She simply hops into the driver's seat, takes a swig of coffee, and starts the engine.

In the trailer, I'm aware of her every manoeuvre. Tyres screech under me and I hear the rattle of dirt and small rocks being eaten up in the exhaust pipe. With no suspension at a speed of 120 km/h, the cushioning provided by the mattress is negligible. With any turn, any small pothole, my whole body jerks up and down in unison with the trailer, and no sleeping position can diminish the effect. Sleep eludes me. All I can do is tuck my knees in close, close my eyes and will the morning to come.

When Jemma pulls up at the quarantine centre, I hop out of the trailer to get some water. I hear someone yell out to me and turn to see a truckie waving in my direction. Truckies driving from Perth to Adelaide have begun to recognise me out on the road.

'I've been seeing you,' he calls out. 'You've quit, have ya?'

The question riles me. I'm standing in this parking lot with an ankle the size of a softball, the glow of Betadine still visible on my shin, where two injection points are concealed beneath a bandage. If Jem looks weary from hours of driving through the night, I look like someone who's been living off the grid for months – rake thin, eyes bloodshot, facial skin blasted by sun and wind. Do I look like someone who's quit? Someone who would *ever* quit? I stare at the trucker, daring him to ask me that again.

It's 2 am when we pull into Madura roadhouse, where Mum hands me a room key. Minutes later, I lie down on the flimsy mattress and coax my body to sleep.

It feels like I've just blinked when Mum wakes me with a gentle shake. It's 5 am. I strap on the dictus band, attach it to my laces.

No one else is out there doing what I'm doing, and that knowledge fills me with pride. There will be no coming up short today. Today, we march on.

35

DAY 15. SIXTY KILOMETRES WEST OF MADURA, WESTERN AUSTRALIA

Much like before, the pain is horrendous. But I lean on my new mantra: if it's not broken, I can run on it. I can find a way through.

Running with the dictus band presents its own challenge. Yes, it helps to alleviate the pressure on my shin, but the swelling is such that I can feel my skin being pinched with each pull of the rubber band. I can't afford to lose any more skin, or have another ailment take hold on this buggered leg of mine, so I stop and grab a compression sock, fitting it over my limb to put some padding between band and flesh.

The route heading out of Madura is hilly, and while the uphill stretches drain life from my legs, it's the downhill ones that prove most problematic. On these, the right-foot strike is too much, and I feel my shin seizing up. I turn my back on the oncoming traffic and try running backwards, which helps a lot. It might look comical to passing motorists, but the tactic ignites a fire in me. *There is always a way through. You just need to find it.*

Sam and Brad follow in the ute, a change-up because Jemma is back at the roadhouse, sleeping off the effects of her valiant effort behind the wheel. I want her out here with me, sharing in this epic three-day rescue mission we seem to have pulled off, beating the odds together. The boys are doing their best, but they have no idea. They haven't learned what I need in these circumstances quite like Jemma has. Rather than trail behind me and stay in communication with truckies to protect my safety, they meet me at a designated spot every five to ten kilometres, ask if I need any food or water, then drive off into the distance, leaving me to chase them.

Mum and Dad arrive at the fifty-kilometre mark, armed with an icepack to wrap around my shin as I force food down and calm my breathing. And then I'm up again, a lonely figure out on the road, nothing but my own thoughts bumping around between my ears, ignoring the plaintive cries of spent fibres.

When I meet Jem at the seventy-kilometre mark, I feel a renewed sense of purpose. We might never have an experience like this again, where the stakes are so high and every minute counts. That Jem is as committed to this as I am makes me only more grateful for her presence. My life is good because she's in it.

When the GPS hits 100 kilometres, I slow my pace and feel a wave of pain flood over me. By now, I'm dragging my right foot again, but the sense of accomplishment outweighs any concern. There was no rest period, no getting comfortable in the time between my last run and the injection; all that mattered was the rush to the hospital, getting treated as quickly as possible, and restarting. With Jemma and Belly having done all they can to get me back on my feet, my commitment to the record has deepened. It's become an obsession that governs my every action.

THE CREW SIT AROUND the dinner table and look up at me as I stumble in, their expressions disbelieving. I meet their gaze with eyes unsoftened by the dogfight that was today's run. I'm still in fighter mode. All I can think is that they have no idea who they're looking at, no idea what I'm capable of.

The crew hadn't said anything to me, but I could sense they'd been worried. I saw the concern that spread across Mum's face when she took in my shin. I sensed everyone's mood change from excited to fearful as they saw the Great Run turning into a miserable walk. *Just over a week into this and already he's breaking down*, they must have been thinking. *What state will he be in five days from now? Ten? Twenty*?

But in the space of a day, I've turned things around, and sitting here at the dinner table, I meet their eyes with a look of cool assurance. *I'm doing it. I will get this done. There is no alternative.*

My body hasn't yet fully adapted to mission requirements, but there's still time. All I can focus on now are the small daily victories, and the sense of hope that pulls me up into each new day. My new magic number, my new favourite number, is 100 – as in 100 kilometres. Each evening when I see that figure and a green tick alongside it, I feel myself itching to go again, to keep proving to myself that I'm capable of more than I ever thought possible.

Later that night, my phone lights up with a text from Belly.

It's a true test of character to see how people show up in hard times. You're showing up mate, I'm proud of you. Let's fucking go!

36

DAY 16. FORTY KILOMETRES EAST OF MADURA, WESTERN AUSTRALIA

The descent into insanity happens gradually. Like a jacket you can slip on and off, I wear it knowingly at first, a kind of mental armour that shields me from thoughts that hit too close to home.

Eventually, however, it sticks. No longer a costume, it's now a uniform I wear daily out there on the road. I used to be able to shrug it off as soon as I hit stop on the GPS, but now it clings to me in roadhouses and keeps me company at night. Sleepless, single-minded to the point of obsession, eyes fixed on the goal with the intensity of a wild animal amid the hunt.

My crew begins to approach me cautiously, their movements contained, their voices low. They don't have to tell me that I'm scaring them. I'm scaring myself, too.

It started with the shin.

The cortisone injection is slow to work, and the pain is now intolerable. There is no respite, no momentary relief from the suffering. From sunup to sundown, all I can feel is a stabbing pain radiating from my knee down to my ankle, pooling at the base of my leg as though I'm standing in flames. This is life in chronic pain: each morning you wake up into the same fits of despair that engulfed you by day's end, and each morning the hope you had for relief diminishes that little bit more, until there is no glimmer, not even a speck, of light visible on the horizon.

Insomnia comes next. Despite the drain of 100-kilometre days, sleep refuses to come. I lie awake groaning, dealing with each muscle spasm, one at a time. The hours pass slowly, then all at once, so that the sound of the alarm shocks. *Surely not again? Surely, I can stay horizontal for an hour longer?*

Nothing is broken, but for how much longer will I be able to say that? I look at my shin and wonder how much more it can take. Is this still the beginning of my adventure, or is it the beginning of the end?

I want to be present, to focus only on the job at hand. But it's becoming clear to me that the potential to do severe damage to myself is real, and I'm forced to ask myself, *Is that a risk I'm prepared to take?* I'm only twenty-three. I'm scared. What kind of future have I signed up for?

I'm turning feral. At this point, I'm focused purely on survival: food, water, shelter – I have no room for intimacy or the small comforts that come with having your partner and close friends in your crew. I'm either pulling away or looking for something to attack – a look, a gesture, a tone, a hidden meaning. I need an outlet for the fear and frustration building up in me. I need a release, and that means taking it out on the people who deserve it the least. Right now, Jemma is in the firing line.

As soon as I snap at her, I know I've gone too far. She's only ever supported me in this madness, and yet I can't bite my tongue. I know I chose to do this, but people don't realise what a lonely place I'm in. Even with the crew close by, I feel vulnerable out on the road, alone with my thoughts.

I've lost the ability to communicate the extent of my pain. A ten rating no longer means much; hyperbole has ceased to exist. I can't bring anyone into my world, so no one can possibly understand what it's like. There's a part of me that wants to push them all away, if only so they might feel the fear that settles over you when you find yourself forever and ever alone.

'What's that look for?' I bark at Jemma.

She looks up at me, her expression soft, absorbing all I throw at her without complaint. She arranges my shoes, prepares my water bottle, assembles my snacks. But I can't stop. My hollow cheeks pull taut across my face, my top lip curls back to expose teeth, and my mouth becomes a kind of volcano, spewing words that Jemma can't outrun.

I watch them engulf her. Jem's face colours and I see everything: first fury, then hurt, then anger and disappointment, until finally all that's left is a crushing sadness pooling in her lash line. Without a word, she goes to the car park and drives off (hopefully to where Mum is parked some twenty kilometres ahead, and not the airport) leaving me to run the next stretch alone.

WHEN I SHUFFLE INTO the aid station Mum has set up, I meet her gaze and feel the years drop from my shoulders. Once again, I'm a child running amok on the farm, a child whose only constraint is the discipline communicated by this mother in a single look. Mum has a way of holding a mirror up to her kids, a mirror that reflects the good and the bad. In her furrowed brow and the straight line of her lips, I see every hurtful word I've spoken in the last two weeks. I see the monster I've become.

'What are we doing out here?' Mum yells. 'Why are we here?'

There's no pushing back, no arguing, just the seeing of truth. I've been consumed by the record, doing everything I can to keep it within reach. It's something the crew understood when coming aboard, but as Mum makes clear, it's not my trip alone. Everyone's made sacrifices. Everyone's dog-tired. Everyone's missing the comforts of home. The difference is, they're putting up with all this for *me*, not for themselves. And, yes, it's humbling to realise that those around you are acting solely out of love, and that their collective decision to give up seven weeks of their lives to drive endless roads in my shadow for the privilege of holding out water bottles and sticks of zinc was an easy one to make. No hesitation, no wavering, just a willingness to lend a hand and be part of something remarkable. At that moment, upon this realisation, the cloud of insanity that had been hovering above me parts and then vanishes.

This run is bigger than me. It's bigger than all of us. Jemma doesn't have to be out here. She could leave at any time. But each day she makes the decision to stay, despite my rudeness, despite my frustration, despite the commands I bark. It's not in her nature to quit, just as it's not in mine. We're a force united in our desire to test ourselves and to clear obstacles others would see as insurmountable.

I run the next five kilometres buoyed by an immense gratitude for everyone who's with me on this journey and the knowledge that there's no airport in any direction for hundreds of kilometres – because if there were, then surely they'd all be on the next flight out.

When I see the ute parked on the side of the road, I walk over to the trailer and find Jemma sitting alone in her thoughts. I give myself over to feeling. I hug her – and it's like coming up for air. All this time I'd felt like I was in rough seas treading water alone, when the reality is Jemma had always been out there in the deep alongside me.

37

DAY 17. TEN KILOMETRES EAST OF MUNDRABILLA, WESTERN AUSTRALIA

I wake up sweating, my chest heaving like an overcrowded jumping castle. Every night I have the same dream, and each time it feels more real . . .

I'm in the teardrop trailer, about to start another day's running, but the pink line of spray-paint marking the previous day's finishing point is nowhere to be found. The trailer keeps moving – back, back, back – onto road I've already run. Finally, Jem and Brad release me from the trailer and I find myself 300 kilometres behind where I should be, and my only choice is to make up all that ground as fast as I can. But it's impossible. I see the record slipping away and Bondi receding so far into the distance that it might as well be in another galaxy. And just when despair is taking hold, I wake up into a new day.

I'm struggling to get going this morning, as if the command to run is being issued in a foreign language. It's all I can do to keep my head down and lean into headwinds that whip at my face. It's just another test, another element looking to see what I'm made of. By the time I lie down on the massage table at the fifty-kilometre mark, I'm at the end of my tether, unable to summon the energy to make polite conversation with the crew.

A van pulls up and a man emerges. Recognition dawns on me slowly. People had been sending me this guy's Instagram profile, a page documenting his training in the lead-up to his attempt at running a distance that's similar to mine. He was starting twenty days after me and I'd wanted to wish him well, but the chance slipped by.

Who knows if it was news of my run that ignited the fire within him to try such a thing? Whatever the case, it hadn't stopped him from tossing a few grenades in my direction – for example, that I hadn't clocked enough kilometres in my training to prepare adequately for what I was trying to do. What's that overused quote? 'By failing to prepare, you are preparing to fail'? True enough. But unless you've run across the country in 40-odd days, yours isn't advice I'm seeking.

There were others, naturally, who questioned my training and voiced doubts about my capacity to endure. But so far, this is the only naysayer who's shown his face. Despite the state I'm in – toes like wilted prunes, a bloated lower leg, out on my feet – I don't want him to see anything in my countenance besides a steely resolve. Say what you want about my training. But don't dare question my conviction to finish what I've started.

The whole time I'm getting rubbed down, he talks about himself. Crew members stand awkwardly around me, unsure of who this guy is or why he's here. When he finally makes to leave to resume his drive west, I wonder if I should thank him – for supercharging the tingle of competition in my fingertips, from where it works its way up my body until it sparks like kindling.

I'M RUNNING INTO THE unknown, my path obscured. I should have more time to play with, but at the eighty-kilometre mark we hit the South Australian border and the clock leaps forward by ninety minutes. It's now 7:30 pm and I have another twenty kilometres to run.

Road trains thunder past. The truckies seem to be growing increasingly displeased by my presence. I guess they reckon I'm in their way and hard to see. With just the single beam of my headtorch and a hi-vis vest, I realise I'm playing a dangerous game. The truckies' patience already tested by hazardous driving conditions, they also need to contend with Jemma's ute trailing alongside me. I howl into the blackened sky, my screams muffled by the sound of road disappearing under monstrous tyres. It's now almost 10 pm and the remaining four kilometres loom like Everest.

Jemma's headlights illuminate the road's fog line. It would be so easy simply to climb into the backseat and keep the watch running while she drives me those final kilometres. It would be so easy to cheat with no one out here to call me out.

But I can't and won't do it – it's a betrayal I would feel, a failure I would never shake off no matter what I accomplished in its wake. Shortcuts, like those opportunities to pull out, present themselves daily. I push on, finding strength in the knowledge that I don't need a referee to tell me to do this by the book. Cheating, like giving up, is not an option.

I think back to the guy who stood over me during my last rubdown, the guy who questioned my smarts and ticker.

I think of the way he sized up my body, took in its battle scars, and had the audacity to ask how I was feeling.

'I have never in my life been better than I am today,' I told him.

38

DAY 19. FORTY KILOMETRES EAST OF NULLARBOR, SOUTH AUSTRALIA

I fear a good day because it means Hell awaits.

Sure, the bad days – when I run without rhythm and each stride seems to rattle my bones – are a test of mettle. On these days, you're drained less by the distance than by the expenditure of the mental energy required to keep going. When you can't claw any sense of hope from the day or muscle your way through, you turn to your mind. It's the only tool you can rely on and, at least so far, it's never failed me.

As masochistic and perverse as it may sound, I've come to relish the bad days. There are never two bad days in a row and to have one is to be offered a rare comfort in certainty. A bad day tells you to keep going, to show up again tomorrow. A bad day tells you something better is on the way.

But today I know I'm in for the worst.

Yesterday was too good, too easy. The Nullarbor was all empty plains. Like running through a commercial for the Australian outback, I found something primal in that landscape, an energy that radiated up from the sun-baked roads, heat dancing across the surface. The thundering bass of Icehouse's *Great Southern Land* sounded in my head. Droplets of sweat ran down my face, pooling in the thick mask of zinc I'd lathered myself in. The 100 kilometres ticked by. I came to the finish and saw Brad waiting for me.

'Are you not entertained?' I yelled to him, both of us beaming.

Neither of us questioned what today might bring. We already knew: destined to be hard from the start.

With no buildings or trees to shield me, I feel the full force of a wind that's stronger than anything I've experienced before. A relaxation of my core muscles, a slight stumble, and I'll be driven backwards. I run two kilometres and feel defeated, a hostage to the cruel conditions you can get on the Nullarbor.

I run over to Jem and Brad in the ute and relay the plan I've hatched.

'This is fucked,' I say. 'I've got to tuck in between the ute and the teardrop trailer. It's the only way I can run through this wind.'

The ute starts up and I sneak a glance behind me to where the wheels of the trailer begin to inch forward, licking at my soles. My challenge is to stay ahead of the trailer while maintaining a safe distance from the back of the ute – essentially running in the one metre gap between the two. For those driving past, I'm a man with a death wish. Truckies on their morning missions are brought almost to a halt, forced to navigate their way past the ute and trailer with me sandwiched in between. I block out the profanities and honks. I'm focused only on Jem, her eyes fixed on my reflection in her rear-view mirror. Occasionally, I holler 'Faster!'

or 'Slower!' as I search for some semblance of rhythm in the turnover of legs and tyres.

A little too much pressure on the accelerator and I feel the wheels of the teardrop clip my ankles. Too little pressure and my head taps the glass of the ute. It makes for a difficult situation for Jem, who can't even rely on cruise control, which won't work unless you're doing at least 30 km/h. The slowness is dangerously sleep-inducing for her. When we finally make it to the twenty-kilometre mark, Jem's body is trembling.

'Nedd's going to get run over – we can't drive like this,' she tells Mum. 'We need something else.'

Okay. Change of plan: I'll try tucking in behind the van instead, it's decided.

Dad hops in the driver's seat and listens out for Mum's commands. Like running on a treadmill with nothing but a blank screen in front of you, all I have to look at is a wall of white, broken only by Mum's face, which watches me attentively in the rear windscreen as she sits in the backseat. I signal 'Up!' with an index finger – which means 'go faster', or 'Down!' ('go slower'). But each time Mum relays the instruction to Dad, he falters. The wind is reducing the van to a toy, and it rattles as if stuck inside a vacuum machine. Dad's struggling to maintain a consistent speed on a single-lane highway with no room for those behind to overtake. It's a nightmare, one not helped by the frequent appearance of road trains. Once they pass, he tries to make up lost time, pressing the accelerator too hard and jolting the van forward. I think I had more fun entombed in the MRI machine.

But for six hours, we keep at it. I feel like I'm running in slow motion. It's like my recurring dream, where I'm dropping ever further back from my starting point, battling across terrain I've already covered. I close my eyes momentarily and feel my weariness, feel the weight of nineteen days and nights on ridiculously inadequate sleep. I give in to it for only as long as it takes Mum to bang on the glass, jolting me back to the present.

AFTER SEVENTY-FIVE KILOMETRES, everyone is wiped. Dad's body is rigid with tension, Mum's face creased with concern. Meanwhile, the wind is only stiffening.

There's nothing left in my body to give. We've tried to find answers, but to keep going into the night the way we are would be to put someone's life at risk.

'How far are we from Bondi?' I ask.

Brad reaches for his phone. 'Two-thousand three-hundred and ten kilometres,' he says.

I do the maths. In terms of the record, we still have twenty-three days before we hit the forty-third day. I'm still in this. It can still be done. But I will *have* to do 100 kilometres a day, regardless of how bad my body feels or how brutal the conditions are. Yep, 100 kilometres is no longer the daily goal. It's the mandate.

I look around at the crew, see their bodies slumped, their heads bowed. Even in these circumstances, stopping for the day feels like a copout, when there's still time to knock out some more kays. But at what cost?

'All right, I'm pulling the pin at seventy-five kays today,' I announce. 'We go again tomorrow.'

No one utters a word of protest.

39

DAY 21. TWELVE KILOMETRES NORTHWEST OF NUNDROO, SOUTH AUSTRALIA

It's palpable among the crew – a sense that the stakes have been raised and every lifeline exhausted.

I'd knocked out another 100 kilometres, as planned, but the conditions had been kind. My crew didn't need to voice their concern; I could see it in their eyes.

When they thought I wouldn't notice, they were taking in my gaunt face and shrinking body, scanning the thin veil of flesh that covered my ribcage, my spaghetti arms.

I understand how they're feeling. Because where could this all lead? If I keep pushing on, will the damage be irreversible? Will I lose a part of myself out here that I will never get back? There is no one around I can ask these questions, much less an oracle who might illuminate the answers.

The morning had been slow, but I trusted the process. I was certain there'd come a time when my body would find a rhythm and my strides would land softer – a brief, gentle touch, not the choppy steps that could be heard a mile off. After a time, I felt muscles unfurl as if waking from a deep slumber. I am still hungry for the record. And finally, it feels like my body understands the assignment and is prepared to work with me.

The incline is gradual, one of those hills that sneak up on you and stretch on for five kilometres. My heartrate climbs and my calves tighten. I feel a tweak in my ankle but push on. It's only when I get to the top that I receive the first shot straight to my Achilles. *BANG!*

I look around for a shooter, someone hidden behind a lone tree or off in the distance somewhere. But there's no one around and no escape vehicle hurtling down the highway, just like there's no blood on me or any evidence of a near-fatal wound. The pain, however, is acute and dizzying, momentarily rendering me incapacitated as I struggle to focus my vision. I take a tentative step, choke down screams that might have broken the bones of my ribcage. Thoughts flood my head. *There's no way. This is not right. It can't be torn. The record. Seventy-six kilometres down. Keep moving.*

I get Belly on the phone and explain what's happened. In just four days from now he'll be back with our crew for the remainder of the journey, having secured time off work. But there's no point denying I need him *now*. I'm aware that since getting the dictus band, it's been pulling my toes up each time my hip lifts. But at the same time as my toes are being pulled up, my Achilles is being pulled down, placing it in this lengthened position on and off for seventeen hours a day. Put simply, it's a disaster waiting to happen. Belly's voice is controlled, and he manages to calm me down by assuring me I haven't snapped my Achilles. Even so, he suspects there's something else going on with it.

I try to keep walking but, after two kilometres, I can't take another step. My danger response is in overdrive, issuing frantic alerts of a threat to survival. So, is this it? I'm now some 2100 kilometres out from Bondi and have just twenty-one days left to get the record. I tell myself it's still possible, remind myself of all those days when my body felt fried, and I could barely summon the energy to tie my laces let alone run. And still I found a way through. Deep down, I can't imagine my Achilles being better tomorrow. I can't see myself running again anytime soon. But I must hold onto hope.

I pass a long night restlessly, and when I finally get back on the road and try to set off, hope deserts me. Each surge of pain in my Achilles feels like an electric shock. The tendon feels as though it could snap at any moment. I've lost the ability to push off the ground, to gain even a fraction of a second's airtime on a stride. All I can do is will myself to walk, each step an act of self-torture. By thirty-four kilometres, I can't move. I'm done.

I message my coach, Matty, updating him on my latest ailment and what it could mean vis-a-vis breaking the record. He'd been analysing my run data and had already noticed a pattern emerging over the three weeks: I was managing two good days of running before my body was faltering and demanding I slow down or stop. And while I was often running through those rough days, they were the danger times for serious-injury risk. For Matty, the solution was simple: go hard on days one and two of a three-day cycle, then pull back on day three. Now Matty proposes a new plan: he wants me to run 116 kilometres back-to-back, then just fifty kilometres on the third day. If I can do that, he says, the record is still possible.

I understand where Matty's coming from, and his plan is simple enough. But while an additional sixteen kilometres mightn't seem like much when you've already run 100, what it would mean for me (and the crew) is hard to contemplate. It would mean another two to three hours out on the road in waning light or none at all; it would mean another two to three hours of dealing with drivers who care far more about reaching their destination as quickly as possible than they do about my safety; it would mean even less time to shovel in food, shower, recover and sleep before doing it all again; it would mean demanding more of a crew that's already toast. It's not just an extra sixteen kilometres. It's a physical and mental chasm no one should be expected to jump over.

Morning breaks, and Jem and I make the drive to Whyalla Hospital for a scan of my Achilles. Mercifully, it's not torn. But the scan finds severe swelling, and when Belly reviews the images, he diagnoses acute tendonitis.

On the drive back, Jem and I talk about everything and nothing at all. The sky turns from blue to pink to blue again as the road disappears in the rear-view mirror. We don't speak about the record, or about how great an inconvenience this day off has been to the pursuit of it. I don't know if I'm nobly holding onto hope or just playing make-believe, but on this return trip I convince myself that everything will be okay. I've been running on no sleep with a right leg that's still getting used to the sensation of the dictus band doctoring its natural movement. I grant myself permission to see today for what it is – a necessary break – and to cut my body some slack.

And besides, maybe I can do 116 kilometres a day . . .

40

DAY 27. KYANCUTTA, SOUTH AUSTRALIA

If there's anything I've learned out here, it's that nothing's guaranteed. Not the weather, not the civility of passing motorists, not the roadhouse amenities. You can't be certain of how you'll feel when you wake up or how you'll fare throughout the day, or when your muscles will run out of juice or when pain will kick like a mule. You don't know whether you'll snap at someone or something or else see your frustration dissolve in a fit of hysterical laughter. And though there'll be moments when you think all hope is lost, you'll invariably surprise yourself, saved by a minor shift in perspective or a small personal victory.

I managed two 100-kilometre days back-to-back, during which I repeated the mantra 'keep pushing'. Matty was right: the third day was when my body blew up. After two days of feeling invincible, I managed just eighty kilometres before breaking down. For just about anyone else, eighty kilometres would be hailed as an accomplishment; for me, with so much at stake and no room for leniency, it registers as a failure.

Messages flood my phone. For every supportive comment there are at least three from naysayers, guys telling me I won't make it, that I should pack it in and come home already. They're the same dismal types who told me I was underdone, who look at my Strava profile and see only numbers; they forget about the most important things: my heart and mind.

Anyone can say they're going to do something, but few are willing to follow through with action. If you're doing it for praise, you'll never make it past the first week. If it's any kind of extrinsic motivation that drives you, you'll wake one morning to lashing winds and feet that feel like minced meat and not have the heart to take one step more. If you're not all-in, if your mission isn't something that occupies your every thought, you're not fair-dinkum. Your heart must be in it, because then you'll understand that the pain of walking away far outweighs the pain you'll experience along the way. Muscles repair. Tendons heal. But disappointment festers into a regret that eats away at your soul.

I think about all that today, which delivers the worst blow so far. There's no sudden injury to one body part, more a fire raging everywhere. I try and get going but my body won't respond. There's nothing to distract me from the multiple sources of agony: severe tenosynovitis in my shins, Achilles tendonitis, blisters that are oozing pus. And now maggots growing in the craters where toenails used to be. What else? Patellofemoral pain. IT-band discomfort. Hip flexors that are completely shot. And biceps that can't straighten for being too long in the flexed position. All unpleasant, all byproducts of this journey I chose to make.

I sit, head in hands, at the twenty-five-kilometre mark, knowing the record is now out of reach. A part of me is shattered: I told myself I'd break it; I made that commitment. But in this moment, I'm overcome not with anger or disappointment but with something else: gratitude. To carry these constant pains is a tangible reminder of the bigger picture. There should be a bolt of lightning as I realise: this has never really been about the record so much as the daily pursuit of something larger – defiance of limitations and negative self-talk; the daily testing of self towards becoming a better person.

No one is making me do this. The option to stop and end this whole operation presents itself every day. With Belly back in the frame, he'd only need to list my interminable list of injuries and people would understand. But my heart is all-in and despite the tomb of pain I find myself in, there's nowhere else I'd rather be.

With the record gone, I could pack up and head home with the crew, but I choose not to. The daily battles between mind and body, the kilometres I power through on nothing but will and stubbornness . . . these matter more than recognition or reward. On this journey, success was never assured. On this journey, as in life, failure intrudes. But there's nobility to be found in continuing to show up, in staying the course no matter what gets thrown at you. *Forget about the record,* I tell myself. *This run is symbolic of the way I choose to live.*

41

Perth is a distant memory, houses and malls a forgotten past. The constant is road trains and other behemoths of the road, thundering along endless stretches of tar. The sun rises and sets, the sky changes colour until it's black. And for all that time, your eyes remain locked on the road in front of you, your legs ticking over but rarely carrying you at a speed that feels satisfying, a speed that gives you a sense of eating into the unclocked kays.

I've run out of games to trick my mind into better ways of thinking. There's barely a change of scenery to draw on, no variation by way of dwellings or shops to shift my focus from the somatic. There are only the sounds of footfall and heavy breathing, occasionally lost on the turbulence of passing vehicles. And then it returns: the near-silence of isolation.

Out here, even the natural world seems stressed, hardened by the realities of life on the Nullarbor and the dusty plains of Australia. Trees may stand erect on either side of the road, but their presence can be more disconcerting than soothing, for leaves cling desperately to dry, skinny branches and bark flakes off like dandruff. Everything that exists here has had to earn its place, has had to fight against those elements that want only to destroy. I feel it, too. Every step forward is a battle, every kilometre a test of will.

Jemma follows alongside me in the early hours, issuing warnings via UHF radio to nearby truck drivers to look out for the lone figure trundling along the fog line in a fluorescent vest. She takes their abuse in her stride, these gruff voices barking down the line, 'This is my fucking road – the bloke shouldn't be on it'.

Lately, though, the truckies have softened. Their voices come over the radio kind and inquisitive. They ask Jemma how I'm doing and where I'm up to. Some have driven from Perth into South Australia enough times now to recognise me. They see the mullet and fluoro pink top combo and toot their horns or yell words of encouragement through open windows. Others pull over to the side of the road, get out and wait for me to come running past, just so they can stand there waving, cheering me on.

While their support buoys me, the interaction is fleeting. I spot them in the distance, get close enough to hear their cries, and then I'm gone, alone once more. I've forgotten what it's like to be surrounded by people. I think about how, at home, I would have to seek out these moments of solitude because they're so hard to come by. In cities, regardless of how early you get moving, you never feel as alone as you do here. In cities, streets might be empty in the early hours, but not for long. There will always be hobby joggers and those walkers who swing their arms in staccato-like movements, and the whoosh of a peloton as lycra-clad cyclists speed past on their bikes, always managing to get so close you can feel their breath on your jawline. But out here, the whole time, excluding people in vehicles, we've seen barely a soul.

The crew and I exist in a bubble. The early mornings disappear beneath routine, before I head to the pink line of spray paint and get on with the job. I don't know what I expected exactly, but in the hours of solitude that follow, I find myself entombed in thought.

I'm walking again, a stiff-legged stagger. It's the best I can manage. I'll walk all day if I have to. I'll walk until the GPS reads 100 kilometres.

I see a mass on the horizon that's moving towards me. Its top half is bulky and wide, while the bottom half teeters on what might be two skinny wheels. It rocks unsteadily in the wind but somehow manages to stay upright. The mass gets closer until eventually I can make out a man hunched over the handlebars of a bicycle. Attached to the bike are two saddlebags and, with their red leather exterior and over-flowing contents, they give the impression of Santa Claus hitting his delivery route early. I hear his heavy breathing as he leans his body left and then right, using the full force of his bodyweight to push down on each pedal. When, finally, he reaches me, he stops and, momentarily, the bike looks like it will tip over, taking him with it.

'How're you going, mate? Where the hell are you riding to?' I say.

In a French accent that sounds almost cartoonish, he tells me he's riding from Adelaide to Perth. He's doing the journey solo and the saddlebags contain everything he needs in terms of food, clothing and tools.

He scans the road behind me to see if I'm being followed, but my crew are waiting several kilometres ahead, likely setting up a quick rest stop for me. I can see in his gaze that he's slightly shaken by this encounter, having likely felt as alone as I have on these outback roads. I tell him about my mission, and his eyebrows rise in disbelief. He doesn't say it, but I can tell he thinks I'm crazy. I want to laugh. Because, to me, running across Australia is simply what I've signed up for. But bike-packing your way from Adelaide to Perth? That's madness.

We chat a bit more, wish each other good luck. Then my French-sounding friend remounts his bike and, with great effort, turns the pedals to get it moving again. I watch him ride into the distance, his calves so big you'd suspect implants but for what he does on a bike. He moves slowly on a narrow stretch of road, and I wonder if he's living every minute with a sense of precariousness, or if he, too, pushes the danger out of his mind to focus instead on what must be done.

Normal people don't venture out here. This is not a welcoming environment for fitness enthusiasts or nature lovers, those looking to take their place calmly amongst the trees as they savour the colours of an Australian sunrise. If you find yourself out here, it's because you're on a mission. You aren't content with being comfortable or treading familiar paths. You're drawn to the extreme, something uncharted; you take a leap into the unknown with little regard for self-preservation. To find yourself here is to have heeded a call. If you're here, you value not security or material possessions but a life of searching, risk-taking, limit-busting. If you're here, you don't covet a social-media following. You crave an adventure into the unknown.

42

Brad can't stop talking about these guys Rich and Andy, two paramotor enthusiasts he and Sam met at the Madura Pass Oasis Motel. Don't be fooled by the name. Whatever the other rooms might be like, I found my room was anything but an oasis. The worn mattress is basically a waste of space; dusty linen evokes a time long past; pillows sit lifeless as if they're yet to be stuffed. Mould lines the bathroom and in the light all you can see are the insects that have been attracted to the glowing fixture, only to crawl in and die. In the rooms and the dining area, tables wear remnants of the previous meal on its surface. Most guests would be on the blower to the front desk. Me? When you've been running for weeks, any place that allows you to get horizontal in passable comfort feels like the Ritz.

When Jem and I were off to get the latest scan, the crew were left at the Oasis Motel with time on their hands. Brad had no sooner sat down outside with a bowl of potato wedges when Rich and Andy pulled out two chairs at the opposite table. As the pair chatted, Brad thought he detected a Yorkshire accent to match his own and, curious, leaned over and asked them where they were from. Turns out, Andy and Brad are a couple of Yorkies. And a shared sense of adventure had landed them here at the same time.

Brad tells me that Andy and Rich were looking to break the world record for travelling from the most westerly point of Australia to the most easterly by paramotor. I'd never seen a paramotor, but it's essentially a motorised parachute that you can steer. Imagine a paraglider. Now picture the pilot with an engine and propeller strapped to their back and you've got a paramotor. The catch, though, is that there's only a certain kind of fuel that can be used in paramotors, meaning Rich and Andy had had to travel the length of their route in a car before beginning their attempt, all just so they could stash fuel along the way in bushes and shrubbery outside gas stations. Unsurprisingly, they've found that some of that fuel has been stolen ahead of their arrival, but the losses so far haven't been heavy enough to derail their plan.

Just as my crew was stuck in limbo while I tried to sort out my body, Rich and Andy had been held up by forces outside of their control. They needed certain weather conditions to prevail to ensure the combination of momentum and safety, but heavy rain and strong winds had forced them to make emergency landings in the bush and then to walk several kilometres, their paramotors in tow, to the nearest roadhouse.

Andy had a welding business back home and his wife had told him he wasn't allowed to buy a super bike because the sport was too dangerous. So, somewhat cheekily, he instead took up paramotoring, through which he met Richard, an enthusiast who aimed to become an instructor one day.

Their trans-Australia dream was running into all manner of delays, which were confining Andy and Rich to various motels for days at a time. But in a show of grit, they weren't giving in. And as tradies they were making themselves useful (and popular), offering to help out in the places they stayed, fixing generators and stuff like that.

Before their Australian adventure, they hadn't known each other all that well, but this trip had bonded them. The experience of flying over mesmerising landscapes, of being pushed mentally and physically, of solving problems while on the move, had turned a casual friendship into something like a brotherhood.

Brad had told them about my cross-country endeavour, about the days completed and the kilometres amassed, about the ever-growing catalogue of injuries that I'd mostly pushed to the back of my mind. How do you explain to those who aren't inside the bubble what it means to be testing your limits? How do you prepare someone to meet a guy who's willing to subject himself to untold suffering? Brad didn't know. He just gave them a warning.

'Listen,' he said. 'Nedd's one of the best blokes you'll ever meet. But when you meet him, he will be a bit off because he's in so much pain.'

Jem and I had driven through the night to get back to Madura. Without even an hour's sleep, I'd laced up and run the requisite 100 kilometres. Let those on social media doubt my ability to make it to the end. Let the haters leave whatever comments brought satisfaction to their humdrum lives. But I wouldn't be listening to them.

When I see Rich and Andy, they're sitting at our table, having charmed the crew with their affable demeanour and quick wit. With my hoodie pulled low over my brow, I sit down and nod in their direction, offering just a guttural, 'Hey, how are ya'.

Turns out Brad was right in his warning: I am off it tonight. Despite hitting my target for the day, I can feel the lack of sleep catching up with me. I don't have the energy to communicate, so I'm obviously not making a winning first impression. Nonetheless, Rich and Andy stick around, asking questions of the rest of the crew and marvelling at my body – specifically the ankle that's so swollen that I can't even wedge my foot into a trainer.

Come morning, we're back on the road, consigning the dank rooms of the Oasis Motel to history. I can feel my body adapting, albeit slowly, and for certain stretches of the day, I'm moving well. The stagger is giving way to longer strides, my arms are working harder. Even my mood has lifted, and the crew and I find moments of levity and laughter amid the barren landscape.

Days pass and the winds ease. When we arrive at the town of Penong, still in South Australia's far west, some 600 kilometres from Adelaide, we're sitting about in the roadhouse, talking about our encounter with Rich and Andy, wondering how they're travelling, when suddenly we see two paramotors circling in the sky before landing, gracefully, on the town racecourse. Our faces light up as they walk into the roadhouse. Finally, as it happens, the weather is on their side, and they've been able to take off and land in the same places they'd stocked fuel.

Over dinner, they tell us about their day, and I find myself getting lost in their stories, which are such a welcome respite from the battle I'm fighting with mind and body. To hear these two guys talk about adventure and thrills stokes my own internal fire. Like the cyclist riding from Adelaide, Rich and Andy are inclined to leave nothing to chance. They know that life offers no guarantees, that things shouldn't be put off until tomorrow, that opportunities must be seized.

Bad weather is rolling in and Andy knows they'll once again be stalled in a roadhouse somewhere. The prospect makes him laugh, mirthlessly, and, turning to Rich, he says: 'This kid with the fucked legs is going to run across Australia quicker than we fly across it!'

Our paths are about to diverge as they head to Byron Bay and we press on along the endless road. But they promise to take off later than us tomorrow morning.

WITH THE EARLY LIGHT covering the landscape in a wash of pale gold, I see a shadow appear on the ground in front of me with the wingspan of a small plane. I crane my neck skyward as I hear the cries coming from above, and that's when I see them, Rich and Andy, making their final farewell. The paramotors dip low so that I can make out their beaming faces. And even as they begin to soar, higher and higher, so that I can no longer discern their features, I can't wipe the smile from my face.

I won't see their finish, and nor will they see mine, but we're rooting for each other. It's something about this region and the people you meet here, so full of life and spirit. With some people, you hold yourself back, dilute your own experiences or play down your lofty dreams, simply because they won't understand, or they'll deem them farcical or the delusions of a madman. But Rich, Andy and I are cut from the same cloth. We're all looking for a life of adventure. And we won't be content until we find it.

43

More days go by, donations continue to flood in. Those voices of doubt and negativity are being drowned out by expressions of support and encouragement. People message me about challenges they're facing in their own lives, about their equivalents of my cross-country run. They tell me that they're choosing to show up for themselves, that they're blocking out the negative self-talk and self-limiting beliefs, that by watching someone like me run for reasons bigger than money, fame, praise, prestige or records, they understand what it is to do something in a pure pursuit of self-improvement. They want to seek their own adventure, to chase their own dreams, to live life in a more fulfilling way. And they want to give generously, in any way they can.

I see that last quality in effect elsewhere. Over the radio, a truckie alerts Jem and others that he'll be pulling over because he's spotted me in the distance. It's as if there's a spaceship on the back of his truck – the sheer size of the thing! Somehow, he wrangles it to the side of the road. Stepping out of the truck, though, the man is unfazed. His face lights up as soon as he sees the crew and me. He shakes my hand with one hand and donates with the other. He doesn't ask for a photo or an autograph, or what he might get in return. He just climbs back into his truck and gets on his way.

Cars pull up constantly. The drivers jump out next to our makeshift rest station, keen for a quick photo and to ask how I'm tracking. For the most part, they're considerate of my energy expenditure and know not to expect my alter ego – the jovial, chatty guy.

I see one car parked some seventy metres down the road, isolated on a narrow shoulder. For five minutes, the doors stay shut, with no obvious movement within. I wonder if anyone will emerge. Perhaps this stop has nothing to do with me. Finally, a man steps out of the driver's side. And I can make out the voice of a young child coming from the backseat.

'Dad, this isn't the playground.'

The dad helps two kids out of the car before the front passenger door opens and his wife (I presume) joins them on their walk in our direction. When he reaches where I'm sitting, I see nervousness etched on his face.

'G'day, Nedd. I'm Tyler. I don't want to intrude,' he says, before pausing. He seems very emotional. Clearing his throat, he continues. 'I can't thank you enough.'

Tyler then tells me about his own struggles in life and how he overcame them. He's followed my run since the beginning and each day he's found something in my journey that's resonated with him. He'd told his son he was taking him to a playground just so he could get him in the car. They'd driven some four hours from Melbourne for the chance to meet me, and all he wanted was to express his gratitude for what I'm doing.

I find myself choking up, just hearing about the impact my run's had on Tyler and how he's trying to influence his kids through his actions and deeds. When he and his family are on their way back to the car, I stop him. I ask whether I can get a photo with him – this man who embodies what it means to do good in the world.

Because to make a difference you don't have to be out on the Nullarbor or the inhospitable roads that meander through Australia's harsh landscape. You don't have to be engaged in a monumental feat of endurance. As Tyler has just reminded me, every one of us faces moments in life that drag us out of our comfort zones. These are the times that challenge us mentally, that cause us to question our abilities, that can leave us rattled and shaken to the core.

Equally, however, each of us has the strength to survive these times – and, more than that, grow and prosper from them. It's the human spirit. We are stronger than we think. You need only open your heart and talk to people to discover there are extraordinary folk who walk among us, even if no one outside their circle knows who they are.

I'M NOW THIRTY-TWO DAYS in and still the finish line feels light years away. Finally, though, our route towards New South Wales peels off the Eyre Highway and the desolate landscape I've been running for so long morphs into a world of life. Farms appear either side of me, the cattle undisturbed by my presence and uninterested in my destination. For so long it had felt like I'd been looking through tinted lenses that muted everything into dull shades of red, orange and brown. Now, a glorious green pushes up from the ground, lush and abundant, and I could almost weep with relief. I want to break into a sprint, to charge at my new habitat with arms extended, to feel the green take hold of me like it does the landscape, imbuing me with vitality. But the truth is, I'm scared.

It's all become so overwhelming. Bad days have continued to accumulate, marked by hours of unrelenting pain. When I'm not running or shuffling, I can scarcely move. Like muscle memory, the pain experienced at these times lingers in my mind. And on the good days, rather than feeling any sense of satisfaction or pride, I have only this fear, rooted in the knowledge that the pain is poised to return. It's pain unconfined to muscle and tendon. It's lurking, surely, deep within my bones. And the longer I dwell in it, the more desperately I want all of this to end.

It feels like I'm in a place that no one should visit for a minute, yet I've made it my home. I stumble through runs grimacing, the inside of my mouth bloodied from where my teeth have clamped down on gums so as to stifle the screams that might otherwise emerge.

I pull up in front of the crew.

'When do you stop? When do you stop doing this to yourself?'

I used to be able to push these thoughts out of my mind, but now they're bolstered by reason: I know I'm damaging myself, possibly beyond repair. But is there something more important than that? There'd better be. Because that shaky conviction is all that's keeping me upright.

I make it to the twenty-kilometre mark and break down. Great guttural sobs heave out from my ribcage; my breathing comes in sharp, shallow gasps.

I look at the bewildered expressions of Jemma and Brad, at the concern etched on the faces of Mum and Dad.

'When does it end?' I plead. *'When does it end?'*

There's nothing any of them can say to me to ease the pain. I know that, and so do they. And so, the loneliness is all-consuming. But just when all seems lost, a text pings from Tom.

Blinking back tears, I open his message and read the words of someone who knows what it means to push so far past your limitations that you find yourself alone on a precipice.

> *Had a dinner today. We enjoyed a roast lamb followed by a dessert I'd made. It was alright. I sat back and let conversation flow for a fair half hour. Then, periodically throughout the course of the four-hour meal, when left unprompted, the group moaned about the work week and their various jobs.*
>
> *Whilst they spoke about that, all I could think was: fuck dude . . . I could walk into every second house and hear the same conversation and be equally as uninspired and uninterested. Someone mentioned a triathlon they'd signed up to and how they dreaded having to raise money for charity.*
>
> *There are fucking levels here . . . Say you then go to another house, say 1 in 1000, where someone tells you about the marathon they once ran, the camping trip they went on, the fact they know someone who rowed across the Atlantic. Say you go to another house, 1 in 10,000, and someone has run an ultra-marathon and runs a marathon or two a year. 1 in 100,000, say someone has swum the English Channel and has Everest on their bucket list.*
>
> *If you can be lumped into a group, no matter the size, what's the fucking point, dude? You've probably heard the*

Rich and Andy flying over me somewhere near Penong. This was special.

This was the end of my fastest 100 kilometres of the whole trip, somewhere outside of Hay, New South Wales. It only took me 9 hours that day, while some days took 17 hours. If only they all felt as good as this.

I had some beautiful messages of support from people along the run, none better than this.

This was day 45 and my third-last day of the run. I ran 106 kilometres this day and I don't think I've ever been more fired up in my life.

Words can't describe how this felt.

At this point I was just trying to take everything in. Finish lines like this don't come around very often.

Mum and Dad holding the banner was extra special.

This was 15 seconds before I drank champagne out of my shoe. It tasted like a million dollars, maybe more.

Upstairs in the North Bondi Surf Lifesaving Club. I don't think we all thought it was real. For so long we were all just trying to make it to Bondi. It was very special to share it with close friends and family.

This is where I finally met Hame, upstairs that night, after all his uplifting, hilarious comments on my daily posts. I am grateful he is now a part of my life.

A powerful beginning to a relationship that will undoubtedly change the world for the better.

This was a pinch me moment, one of very few childhood dreams of mine that have actually come true. Thanks, Jimmy, for allowing me to feel like a rockstar for three minutes.

Since the end of the run, I've been fortunate enough to rub shoulders with some very cool people who I hold in high regard, none other than these three. *Top left:* Israel Adesanya. *Top right:* David Goggins. *Bottom:* Rich Roll.

My first keynote in front of 3000 people in Melbourne. What a fun way to get uncomfortable. It was a fun way to get over your fear of public speaking.

yarn 'most people die when they're 25 but we don't bury them until they're 80'. I think it's more like most people are born in a mass grave and never try to get out. At the end of the day, we are only as good as our stories and the impact we have on others.

Over half a million dollars soon to become one million. Running across the most ominous landmass on the planet. Inspiring a nation. Redefining resilience. Redefining what's possible. Redefining sanity. Go talk about the south of France. Go talk about your park run. Go talk about how awkward it is to raise money for charity. Go fuck yourself. You're here to live, brother. And some people will just never understand.

Goosebumps prickle my skin. How lucky I am to have someone like Tom in my life, how lucky that we somehow found each other during the fifty marathons, forging a bond over a desire to live life to its fullest. He doesn't deliver empty platitudes or token catchphrases. You know the ones. *Pain is inevitable, suffering is optional. A journey of a thousand miles begins with a single step.* Please. Just please. It's enough to make you want to throw your phone at a wall.

Tom's words resonate because they're words he lives by. And so, I know I'm not alone out here.

For the past four weeks, I'd been consumed with thoughts about the run and its impact on my body. These thoughts live rent-free in my mind, but there's only so much real estate up there and as they've piled higher, one atop the other, pressure building, it's been a case of waiting for an implosion.

As usual, Tom's words cut through the noise. I'm reminded to focus and return to first principles – to the *why* of life.

It's the reason I'm still out here clocking 100-kilometre days even though the record is now out of sight.

This isn't about me or the record. It's about inspiring action by doing. It's about giving. It's about choosing to live life to the full, knowing nothing is guaranteed, that it can all be snatched away in an instant.

44

DAY 36. FIFTEEN KILOMETRES WEST OF CULLULLERAINE, VICTORIA

In a trance, I stumble into a jog. Fog hangs in the air, coating the landscape like a blanket. You can barely see a metre in front of you. I register the beep of the GPS, alerting me to another kilometre completed, but it feels like I've disassociated from my body and these arms and legs are moving of their own accord. If it weren't for the thumping of my heart, I'd assume I was dreaming.

I keep seeing my phone light up, but I can't work out what kind of notifications I'd be getting out here. Reception, which has been patchy at best throughout the journey, might finally be kicking in, and perhaps this is where I'll be brought up to speed on what's been happening in the world I used to occupy.

When I get around to checking my messages, I realise there's no way I can get through them all. It's not just check-ins from friends and family. Everyone from shopkeepers to running enthusiasts are following my journey, and many among the latter are in Mildura, the large town in northwest Victoria on the banks of the Murray River, and they want to run with me. I've been posting on Instagram throughout, providing updates on my body and our progress across this wide brown land, but I never expected anything like this. But what to make of it? With phones, comments come in and every so often the floodgates open with likes, but it never feels real. It's just this bizarre, ersatz world that exists wholly within your device. You can't see it or feel it, and so you wonder whether people will do what they say. Will they really be cheering for you when you need it most?

Just shy of 100 kilometres, I spot a motor inn on a quiet street, Springfields on Deakin. The manicured grass out front holds the kind of allure you'd expect of a luxury villa: serenity and comfort, the most inviting few square metres you could imagine.

Tentatively, I lay my body down, allowing myself to think about Bondi. We now have fewer than 1000 kilometres to go. I have steered clear of viewing the run as a distance to be covered. To have thought of it that way would have been self-defeating, I figured, because the distance is simply too great, too daunting to get your head around. I broke it down into those (vaguely) manageable daily blocks of 100 to keep myself out of the nearest psych ward. But now that I'm quite close to Bondi – not really, but relatively – I give myself permission to daydream. We're so close I can almost feel the cool sea breeze on my face – until the sound of a car horn yanks me from my reverie.

Back on the road, it's like a Thanksgiving Day Parade. On both sides, drivers and passengers lean out of their windows, waving vigorously to catch my attention or yelling words of encouragement. Others simply stare in disbelief, while others still film me on their phone cameras.

I look to Jem and Brad for some insight into what's going on, but their expressions are as bewildered as my own. One driver recognises me as they drive past and, within minutes, they've circled back and parked precariously, all so they can snap a picture.

When I look to Brad, a grin stretches across his face as he takes his phone out and points it at me, as if I'm suddenly a celebrity and not someone he's watched defecate on an off-road makeshift toilet for the past five weeks.

It feels like we've gone through a portal into another world. Since Perth, interactions out on the road have been few and fleeting. The bubble encapsulating the crew and I has housed profound conversations and comedic observations; together, we've generally been able to find levity and humour in even the darkest times. We never thought word would spread to such an extent that people in Mildura would be hanging out of their car windows to engage with me. A mission that I thought might capture the attention of a few has grown bigger than I could have imagined. People might want a photograph and a quick word, but mostly they want to donate to the cause. As wallets are fished out of bags and pockets are emptied, the people of Mildura prove there is no limit to our capacity to give.

45

I'd thought the silence would return, that it would again be just me and the sound of footfall on bitumen. But since crossing the Victorian border, the crowds have been constant. Indeed, the number of well-wishers on the sidelines is only increasing, while from out their window drivers wave cash or much-needed fuel in the form of an energy drink or chocolate bar.

Even those who stand awkwardly alongside an enthusiastic partner or sibling mostly wear an expression of intense curiosity. They might not have a clue who I am or what I'm doing, but the DIY signage hanging from rubbish bins and other fixtures, coupled with the rowdy cheering, has created an atmosphere one can't simply walk past. It's the kind of support you'd expect for a national team arriving home with a prestigious trophy in tow. Only in this case it's just me, sporting a bleached mullet and weathered hat, getting all the attention.

The closest I'd ever come to this kind of fuss was in Centennial Park after the fifty marathons, when friends, family and fellow running enthusiasts showed up in numbers.

But country folk produce a different atmosphere entirely. In various towns, 500 people will line the main drag, and where there's no petrol station or parking lot to accommodate everyone, parked vehicles will line both sides of the road, and on these vehicles they will stand, hooting, hollering and waving cans of beer as I run past.

In Hay, set on the Murrumbidgee River in southwestern New South Wales, I receive a text message from a woman whose mother owns an Airbnb on the river, inviting the crew and I to stay a night there free of charge. Having bounced around between countless roadhouses, with communal toilets emanating odours so pungent they singe the nostrils and turn the stomach, we accept this kind offer without hesitation.

When we arrive, weary beyond measure, we can't believe our luck. If the picturesque setting and river location aren't enough, there's even a Jacuzzi to soothe my aching muscles. Later, we all sit down for a lamb roast, part of a spread that leaves you wide-eyed, unsure which dish to dig into first. On the owners' part, there's no expectation of receiving anything in return; their hospitality is born purely of kindness and generosity.

As we edge closer to Sydney, and the towns get bigger, more and more people are lining the streets to watch me run past. In each place, James runs around with a bucket, collecting donations. In Wagga, we manage to raise $5000 in cash. I wonder what it is that compels people to be so generous, but maybe their faces say it all. They simply want to be part of something good and meaningful; they're hungry for a sense of decency in a world that too often seems to have lost its way. Here's me running across Australia, raising money for the homeless. And they admire that. But that doesn't mean they'd ever contemplate some crazy physical pursuit of their own. Perhaps they're simply trying to find the courage to start a conversation with someone new, or to read a book, or simply to look up from their phone and meet the eyes of the person sitting opposite on the bus, to taste a moment of shared experience, shared understanding. I think of Tom and his words of encouragement and the donations flooding in. I think of the homeless I met around Sydney's Central Station and the misery they live with.

Never does the running become smooth, automatic. Sometimes it's relatively painless; mostly, I feel hostage to a body that refuses to comply. My hips and knees are on fire, and I can feel the pull of every tendon below my navel. Negative thoughts are inextinguishable – thoughts of failure, concerns around the toll this must be taking on my body, disquiet about the work I left behind in Sydney that left me unfulfilled and craving a challenge. For weeks I've been screaming for this all to end. But I know that as soon as it does, I'll think back to these days on the road and find myself nostalgic for the pain, for it, as much as anything, makes me feel alive.

46

DAY 46. MARULAN, NEW SOUTH WALES

At our Airbnb, the alarm sounds at 3:30 am. I wonder if I should feel a sense of relief, knowing this is the last time for quite a while I'll have to pull myself up into the predawn and command my body to action. But there's no time for reflection. We discussed the plan last night: get to Campbelltown by nightfall, leaving just sixty kilometres for me to run on the last day. It'll allow for something of a sleep-in for me and the crew tomorrow, when I'll make my way to Bondi's finish line.

Yep, if I can just get to Campbelltown before dark, then the last day will be something to savour.

Still, today is another call to battle. In the bathroom, I lock eyes with my reflection. My cheeks are now hollow, two shadowy streaks on an otherwise sunburned face. My lips are cracked and blistered. My arms protrude like two matchsticks from a shirt that hangs loose on my frame, like a tarp billowing in the wind. Every part of me is smaller than when this began. If it wasn't for my eyes and the bleached mullet, I'd be unrecognisable – even to myself. But I stare at those eyes in the mirror, eyes alarming in their focus, unwavering in their concentration; the eyes of the hunter not the hunted; steady, certain, fixed on their prey. I switch the light off and head out to the starting line with the crew. *Just one last fucking day of running big, big kilometres Let's go.*

Hours later, the sun sits high in the sky, but the air is crisp, refreshing like a coastal breeze. I can almost hear Bondi's siren call, luring me in.

I'm moving well. There are dull aches and the occasional sharp, acute pains that persist deep within bones, but we're close now. The end is in sight. To succumb to the pain now would be more than just foolish – it would be an insult to the crew and the sacrifices they've made daily to help get me this far.

Now, the end is near. I run across bridges where signs are stretched across railings, my name written in permanent marker or acrylic paint, and along the shoulder of the Hume Highway I see scores of chalked messages, usually some variation of *We'll see you in Sydney*! These anonymous exhortations, from people I've never met and will never be able to thank, touch my heart.

But what brightens my mood more than anything is the familiarity of my surrounds. Throughout my journey, we've used maps to tell us where we are and the distance accumulated. But these undulating roads I'm running now are familiar to me. I'd travelled them years before when I was making frequent trips between Sydney and Canberra. I see truck stops I've rested in, service stations that have been a godsend on a near-empty tank. I know these roads. And now they're leading me home.

When I get to the twenty-kilometre mark for a rubdown on a stretch of the Hume Highway, I see my disbelief mirrored on the others' faces. Against all odds, we've somehow made it this far. I lie on Belly's massage table, and he kneads my hips while Mum and Dad focus on my calves and feet, and Jem rubs my head. I'm probably wallowing in it a bit – this extravagant display of care and attention – but it's the last time for a long while I'll be getting this kind of treatment, so who can blame me?

The mood in the camp is buoyant and swells with the cacophony of street noise. We're like kids at school camp, our dialogue defined by shorthand communication and in-jokes. We know the memories we're creating will last a lifetime.

James meets us out on the road. Perhaps sensing our bewilderment, he talks to us with a fatherly calmness. He's trying to prepare me for tomorrow in Bondi, where he suspects the turnout will be big. Just how big, it's impossible to say. I know what he means. I can't even picture what tomorrow may look like at the finish line. All of that is outside my control. And I'm still in battle, after all. I have just one question.

'James, what's the second record? What's the second-fastest time for crossing Australia?'

His lips curve into a smile as he meets my gaze. 'Forty-seven days and one hour,' he answers. 'Some bloke known as the godfather of ultrarunning.'

I can't suppress my joy, knowing I've got him beat. 'Perfect. I'm Daddy, then.'

I move through the landscape like a well-rested man, my strides no longer short and choppy. Above me, light leaks out of the sky until the pastel shades of pink and blue are replaced with the greys and blacks of evening. It's already 7 pm and I still have another fourteen kilometres to cover on top of the 100 I've already managed today.

I don't want to have to come back to the highway tomorrow morning. It's dangerous to be running this late and it leaves little time to recover tonight. But I know if I can just make the Narellan Road turn-off to the south-west suburbs of Sydney, I'll be in a good headspace come the final run. I slip on my hi-vis vest and headlamp – hopefully for the last time – and watch as the few stars above are obliterated by its harsh glare.

Shiver-sweating in the darkness, I don't feel so alone. As Sydney gets closer, so too does the stimulus that surrounds me. For so long, it's been just me and the crew, isolated yet mostly content in our bubble. For the past forty-six days, it's seemed as though the reality outside this bubble had ceased to exist. We had created our own world in which we didn't think about our previous life – about rent or work or all the petty concerns that usually clog our heads. Nor did we think about the future. We couldn't: the present demanded our attention. All we could think about was how we were going to get through *today*, dealing with challenges as they arose. It's been exhausting. A herculean effort from everyone. And amidst the suffering and sacrifice, we had moments of eye-watering clarity. These emerged from long talks or the fact of venturing into the Australian outback and marvelling at its beauty, knowing all the while that it was there, in the nowhere regions of our colossal land mass, that our lives changed fundamentally forever.

IT'S AFTER 8:30 PM WHEN I finally stop my watch after 114 kilometres. It seems certain now: tomorrow will be my last day. Tomorrow, this will end. I'll need to run sixty kilometres to the finish.

I consider what that, finishing, will be like, what it will mean to have achieved something I dreamed into action more than two years ago. Will I be exultant? Or will I be aware of losing something in the act of completion? Will I learn that it is indeed better to travel hopefully than to arrive?

James has managed to find the only restaurant still cooking this late on a Sunday night in Campbelltown. Also, a spa bath has been set up for me courtesy of Budgy Smuggler. I sink into the water and feel my muscles surrender to the heat. It's hard to fathom that we're here, harder still to believe that forty-six days in, having suffered all manner of injuries, I managed my biggest run of the whole journey on the penultimate day.

I see James go over to Mum, who's sitting outside her hotel room.

'How's it been?' he asks.

At once, tears start running down Mum's face, as though a pipe has burst. My guess is they're tears of relief and exhaustion. None of us ever dared question my ability to get this done, but now that we're here, none of us can comprehend that it's almost over. Perth feels like a lifetime ago. Looking at Mum, I can see how the grind of watching me linger in the fires of hell has aged her in the space of seven weeks. But now the end is coming so fast.

Belly gives me a final rubdown before I hit the mattress, my eyes already half closed. With just sixty kilometres to run tomorrow, there's no need to set the alarm for 3:30. I feel the warm arms of sleep embrace me and fall into them.

47

DAY 47. CAMPBELLTOWN, NEW SOUTH WALES

A series of bangs shocks me awake and for a few moments, all I can do is lie here, dazed. I sit up and scan my hotel room: there's no culprit to be found. I rub sleep from my eyes and try to make sense of my surroundings like a stunned reveller in a drunken stupor. There's a pounding in my head I can't shake. It feels heavy, like I'm wearing an invisible tyre as a hat. Just then, the door opens and Mum walks in, a puzzled look on her face.

'Has anyone else got a headache?' she asks.

Through the open door, I see someone moving. Then Belly emerges, his face weary beyond description.

'Man, I've got a raging headache,' he announces.

I look at my watch on the nightstand. It's 7 am – the biggest sleep-in we've had across the whole journey. It's more than three hours past what has been our standard waking time, at which point we've been slamming down four shots of espresso to launch us into the day. Now, caffeine withdrawal symptoms have whacked us in our sleep.

The problem diagnosed, none of us hesitates. There's a coffee machine on the counter, sleek and functional. But good coffee takes time and right now, we just need the caffeine in our systems.

So, we grab a jar of instant Moccona and start scooping it into mugs, then pour boiling water over the brown pebbles and watch them dissolve, our cue to gulp down the black and glossy liquid. Who knew seven weeks could turn us into a bunch of caffeine addicts?

I'd have expected last-day nerves, but in the hotel room the vibe is pure excitement. Jem and I weigh my outfit options for the final run, knowing that whatever I choose will be immortalised in our memories. What does an occasion such as this call for? Fluorescent pink, orange or yellow? In what I think is a tasteful choice, we opt for the pink.

In the scheme of things, sixty kilometres feels almost like a treat, a rest day if you will. But the fact is it's a sizeable distance, one that will still prove challenging regardless of how seasoned your legs are or how primed for endurance you've become. Despite the extra hours of sleep, my body feels stiff as a plank.

Nonetheless, as I head out to the day's starting mark, I feel the same keenness to get going as I did back in Perth. It's all happening. It's the last day. It's time to finish what I started.

The streets of Campbelltown seem narrow; they're choked with traffic. There's no way for Jem to safely trail alongside me in the ute, nor Mum and Dad in the van with the teardrop trailer. So, we agree on various meet-up points along the way, but mostly I'll be running and navigating the streets alone.

I turn on Google Maps and keep glancing at my phone as it directs me towards Bondi. Mistakenly, it's set to walking routes, which are sending me up train-station stairs and through various parks, adding hundreds of metres to my journey as though scenery is my priority. There's no more stopping on the side of the road to relieve myself, not with the people of Lakemba out and about, many keen to get a glimpse of the mullet blowing in the wind.

Twenty kilometres into the run, I meet Jem at a service station and see her smile stretch wide. After all we've been through along the way, we're still doing it, and we're doing it together. I want to savour this moment, and file it away somewhere in my brain to draw on later. But I hear my name being called and turn around to see a journalist and a videographer poised for action. I don't know how they've managed to find me but here they are requesting an interview, blind to the fact I've still got another forty kilometres to run and have no energy to spare.

Jem dismisses them calmly, telling them simply that I won't be doing any interviews until this is over. And when they clock the determination in my eyes, they don't put up a fight, retreating out of the service station and out of sight.

I didn't know what to expect today in terms of media interest. I thought maybe the concluding stages of my journey might generate some online news coverage, but I didn't anticipate news crews, working off tips as to my whereabouts, trying to follow me to the finish. Jem and I look at each other, knowingly. This is only the beginning.

I shoot a message to James, ask whether he can arrange a hotel room or private space where the crew and I can meet up before the last few kilometres. We need somewhere to shelter from the building chaos. Everywhere we turn, pedestrians are congregating on street corners and footpaths, their phones held aloft, their screams of encouragement unintelligible. Cars are darting around me, their drivers intent on snapping photos. Any sense of calm we felt this morning has evaporated.

Following the route on my phone, I run northeast on Canterbury Road and see street signs directing me to Parramatta Road, which will usher me into the city. I know that once I reach Parramatta Road, I'll have just thirteen kilometres to run to get to Bondi. Thirteen: a number that seems bafflingly tiny in the context of recent weeks.

Right now, though, the key number is thirty.

Thirty kilometres, I tell myself. *Thirty more kilometres and you're done. That's three hours of running.*

I crest a hill and see something amazing on the horizon: Sydney Tower, the Harbour Bridge, towering skyscrapers. *Holy shit.*

I run into the Garden Lodge motel on Parramatta Road where James has managed to book us a room on short notice. Staff buzz around us looking nonplussed, no doubt wondering why this disparate group of pilgrims would book a room for a night with the intention of staying only a couple of hours.

In our room, Belly has his massage table set up while Mum and Dad are laying out food. With a chicken wrap and apple turnover on my plate, I sit down and take out my phone.

5.30 pm. Bondi. Shut her down, I post to my Instagram. *Don't be late.*

48

It's obvious on the massage table that my back has seized up, a consequence of undulating roads and how I've been bending my neck to follow directions. For forty-five minutes, Belly tries to release the tension, subdue the spasms. He's been doing this kind of thing for so long now, with such intensity, that it's a miracle he doesn't have RSI in his wrists.

With the plan to reach Bondi at 5:30 pm, we have some time to kill in the hotel. You'd think we'd appreciate the breather, but the hours pass slowly, and all of us look and feel agitated. Any sense of calm we felt out on country roads is gone, knocked out of us by car-horn blasts and demanding news crews.

Brad pipes up.

'It's going to be one of those events where you go, "Where were you when Nedd Brockmann ran into Bondi?"'

I look at him, expecting a ribbing or some sarcastic adjunct to punctuate the remark. But he simply looks at me steadily, and in that moment, we both realise the magnitude of the day. For seven weeks we've been at war together, and now we're headed home, victorious.

I can't quieten my phone, which is pinging like a one-armed bandit. Messages are pouring in from friends and strangers; notifications alert me to the thousands of tags I'm getting on social media, where you can see the crowd building at Bondi hours ahead of my arrival.

Seeing this, most of the crew take it as their cue to leave; they'll need to go ahead and set up the finish. For me, it's hard to imagine they won't be close by over the remaining few kilometres, that there'll be no hand waving a drink at me, no one assembling the portable toilet on the shoulder of a road. Instead, theirs will be the faces I'll search for in the final metres.

Brad picks up his camera. 'We'll see you down there,' he says, turning to go with most of the crew, leaving just Jem and Belly in my company.

When it's finally time for me to go, the stiffness has returned to my body, so now I'll need to warm up before setting off on this final stretch.

When I step outside the hotel and back onto the street, I see a familiar face. It's Declan, a good friend, who tells me he's been sitting out here on his moped for the last two hours or so, having tracked my location on Find My Friends. He takes in my gaunt face, swollen ankles and battered knees, and I see shock pass over his face like a shadow, only to be replaced by joy when he looks into my eyes.

I can tell by his expression that the question he wants to ask is: *How the fuck are you here?* And the truth is, I wouldn't know how to answer him. The things we've faced, we shouldn't be here – that we are defies all logic and reason. But Declan's known me long enough to understand that, with me, there was never a choice. Finishing is the only option.

With Declan trailing on his moped, I run through Petersham and Moore Park. It feels like every second car is honking at me. People are dangling out of passenger windows, pumping their fists, urging me on.

But as I run through Ultimo, I see people with their heads down, gazing at screens or newspapers, standing in line for their coffee, making polite conversation. They walk by oblivious to my presence, focused on what's going on in their own lives: a work meeting, a family dinner, that grocery list left behind on the kitchen counter. To these people, I'm just another stranger, another bloody runner hogging the footpath. No matter the scenes down at Bondi Beach. Here, just a few kilometres away, I'm nobody.

We all want to think we're special, that our achievements deserve recognition, that our legacy will outlive us. Despite the heady scenes awaiting me, I remind myself that people seldom dwell for long on any one feat or event, no matter how remarkable it may be. New marks are set and broken. People move on.

When it comes to creating a legacy, I tend to think that more important than what you've done is *how* you do it – how you managed yourself in those moments that rattled your psyche and challenged your deepest-held beliefs. As I near Bondi, I think of all the donations that have come in, all those people who've given so generously along the way. More important than any achievement or accolade is the integrity with which one lives, the striving to do good in this world. When it comes to the vast and varied fabric of the human experience, kindness is the greatest blessing we have to give.

Just when I'm dwelling on all this, I turn onto Eddy Avenue and there I see those dreadlocks that caught my attention once before. It's Dave, the first homeless guy I went up to almost three years ago. Goosebumps rise on my flesh as we lock eyes.

'Hey, Dave! How are you?'

He beams. 'Hey, Nedd!'

We salute each other as I continue down the same avenue on which I walked to TAFE, the stretch that changed my life because it was here I connected with the homeless. It had to be this place. I had to return to where it all started, knowing that the money I'm raising is going to help Dave and countless others like him.

When I hit Anzac Parade, I feel like a popstar who's been sighted by his most zealous fans before a show. Stunned faces greet me as people run frantically behind, phones out, of course. Cars pull up as curiosity blankets both sides of the road. Even those pedestrians who have no idea what's going on look suddenly intrigued, and they're soon enough reaching into their pockets for their phones. They're unsure of what it is exactly they're filming, but in case you hadn't noticed, you and I are back in a kind of Wild West: shoot first, ask questions later.

I see Jem's car at the Olympic Hotel in Paddington, where she and Belly signal for me to meet them as Declan provides a buffer between me and the trailing crowd. When I open the car door and hop in, I take what feels like my first breath in hours. Jem cranks the volume as Avicii's *Level*s blasts over the stereo, but there's a distinct buzzing sound that can't be attributed to the bass alone. We get out of the car and look skywards. There are two news helicopters circling above, cameras locked on our every movement like this is an episode of *Australia's Most Wanted*.

'Holy shit,' Belly gasps. 'This is going to be bigger than *Ben Hur.*'

Jem is frantic. 'What if I need to go to the toilet at Bondi? I can't miss the finish, Nedd! I need to go now.'

She darts inside to use the hotel facilities. Less than a minute later, Belly follows suit. When they emerge, we know it's time. I'll be running the final five kilometres alone.

'Are you sure you're going to be okay?' Jem asks.

I nod. 'This is it. Let's do it.'

'We love you, mate. We'll see you down there,' says Belly, before hopping in the car.

I watch them drive off, gratitude rising again. A sense of freedom envelops me. And when I start running, I feel all but weightless, my feet touching the ground with the briefest and lightest of touches.

Through Bondi Junction I run, feeling the air turn cold, salty, a familiar ocean breeze you can taste on your tongue. I feel invincible, any pain masked by elation and relief.

I think I hear Declan say something from his bike, but when I turn around, he's only smiling and directing my eyes to the front with a swift nod. I look then and see it. People clustered on pedestrian islands and around traffic lights, huddled on street corners and in bus shelters, squeezed like sardines into any available space.

'Oh, my God – you're here,' one says over a chorus of 'Well done, mate!'

When I get to the top of Bondi Road, I see a field of yellow hi-vis vests before me, and beyond that a colourful tapestry of faces blinking in the distance. Police officers approach me with ebullient faces, stopping the crowds as they usher me across the road.

I can't believe it. Who shuts down Bondi Beach? The Queen? Justin Bieber? But a kid from Bedgerabong? You'd never believe it. I can see the crowd swarming along the esplanade, its tail stretching into the distance. People are dashing in from everywhere. It seems to be no longer a question of if you want to go down and watch this character; it's a case of, *Get me there*!

There are now more people at Bondi Beach than I've ever seen before, and that's counting the most sweltering days of the hottest summers. But the beach itself – the sand and waves – is practically empty. Everyone's lined up for me on the esplanade, chanting my name as though it's a war cry. A sense of imposter syndrome invades my head. *Why have so many people bothered to show up? I shouldn't be pulling a crowd like this.*

A police officer approaches me cautiously, conscious of my shell-shocked look.

'Are you good to go, mate?'

I scan the heaving crowd. Looking back at the officer, I'm unable to contain the tears welling in my eyes.

'I don't know,' I say.

49

I glance down at my watch: 5:15. I'm fifteen minutes ahead of schedule.

'I'm early,' I tell the police officer, who looks baffled – and fair enough. It's not every day that the streets of Bondi get closed off to vehicles just so some bloke can finish his run. Does punctuality really matter at a time like this, or should I just get on with it? I fire off a message to Mum, who's with the crew on the esplanade, waiting for me.

Mum! I'm here and ready to go. Am I too early?

Her reply is almost instant. *Can you just wait five minutes and then head down?*

The police officer flashes me a smile. 'It's fine, mate. Do what you've gotta do.'

He shepherds Declan and me to a little street just off the main road. We're almost laughing now at the circumstances, knowing things are only getting more chaotic as more people cram into the area around the finish line.

Sitting there, I try to catch my breath, but those who followed me along Bondi Road know where I am, and Declan is having to serve as a bodyguard to keep me from being mobbed by a stampede of excited followers.

It feels like days pass in the space of those five minutes, during which there's no meditation, breathwork or visualisation. There's just my heart, pounding against my chest like an animal trapped in a cage.

Finally, I turn to Declan and the police officer.

'Righto. Good to go.'

I hear my words repeated into the policeman's walkie-talkie, followed by the sound of static and then raucous cheering. As I run out of the side street and onto the main road, I can barely see anyone clearly as tears cloud my vision. All I hear are cries of encouragement coming from every direction. 'Go, Neddy!' they cry.

Fists are pumping. Phones are everywhere, pointed at me, and behind them are sets of eyes crazy with excitement.

I can't work out what's happening – this crowd of cheering fans making for too surreal an experience for my addled brain to make sense of. But I do feel a sense of pride, as well as a renewed awareness that this is a big day, one that many people will never forget.

Just before I hit the esplanade, I see a wall of cops and there, parting the crowd, is a buggy with Brad, Jemma, Belly and Sam onboard. The wheels are practically deflating at the weight of them all on the tiny backseat. Their eyes are locked on me, their expressions exuberant. They're among the only ones who know what I've been through to get to this moment, who understand the depths I've plumbed over the last forty-six days. The crowd might be cheering my name, but the fact I'm here is just as much the crew's achievement as mine.

Jem beams at me as the wheels spin and they edge down the tunnel of people towards the finish, where a banner reads:

Welcome Home Nedd, You Crazy Motherfucker

I tell them to drive faster as I go to run the final metres of this epic journey, turning back once more to view the crowd that has gathered at the top of Bondi Road. I beckon with my arm – *Come on! Come down* – and as they take my cue, I turn and head into the crowd.

The chants get louder and louder until it feels like we're in a stadium. People lunge forward with their arms outstretched, elated to be a part of something special. I can't make out any faces. I thought time might slow down about now, that the detail of every moment might be starkly rendered. I thought I would make out every face, that my mind would realise the significance of such an occasion and know to take it all in. Instead, everything passes in a blur. I see only a sea of people huddled either side of the buggy, the narrow chute squeezing smaller and smaller like a pressure valve, so that it could implode at any moment. And all I can do is scream. Elation works its way through my torso and up my spine. It rips out of my chest and leaves me momentarily weightless, invincible. And when I cross the finish line, my excitement is such that I feel like I haven't run at all.

50

And there it is: 3953 kilometres in forty-six days and twelve hours, and $2.6 million raised for We Are Mobilise. The start feels now like both a lifetime ago and yesterday.

The crew jumps off the buggy and embraces me, and then I see Mum and Dad, holding the finish-line banner. As they hug me, I let the tears fall. We went through it together. It wasn't just me – it was *our* Bondi run.

Turning to look at the crowd that hasn't stopped screaming since I first appeared at the top of Bondi Road, I see just how big this run became, and how many people were inspired. All the pain has been worth it.

James approaches me, beaming with pride. As journalists and news crews rush up to me, James places a protective hand across my back and steers me away. Amid the chaos, he is an island of calm. This run may have connected us, but I know now that his purpose in my life exceeds this endeavour alone. For me, he's a family man who's always available to talk, always willing to drop everything to come to your aid. I'm not a member of his family, but our bond is more than just collegial, based as it is on a shared energy and a shared desire to change the world through action. With James by my side as I fumble through a couple of interviews – mostly incoherent in my post-run daze – I can feel only a deep gratitude for this man who's come into my life.

James ushers me up the stairs to the North Bondi SLSC and into the office. I spend half an hour sitting there with Jemma, both of us trying to absorb the last hour or so. When I pull my phone out, there's no service, the crowd that's gathered having drained Bondi of all its 5G. As I walk into the after-party, there's an eruption from my close friends and family.

Right now, no part of me is feeling the effects of those 3953 kays. It's like I've been reborn with new hips, fresh legs and a better-than-ever back. I'm not even tired. The effects of weeks of sleep deprivation seem to have been wiped out, though more likely my brain is secreting a dopamine rush of such epic proportions that I don't dare imagine what the comedown will entail.

The celebrations continue into the night. Finally, guests start heading home and, eventually, just the hard core remains: Sam, Belly, Brad, Jem, James, Mum and Dad.

The room fills with emotion as we scream out the lyrics of classics from AC/DC and Jimmy Barnes. We've all suffered together but also laughed and learned and found beauty in the strangest things. There were times that must have changed us, though, those days when I woke up screaming in agony and the thought of having to put one foot in front of the other was too much. The crew were there for it all.

I think back a couple of years, to when I invited these people to come along on this crazy journey I was planning. Excitement had bubbled up in all of us. These are the people who know me as no one else does. What do they know? That I finish what I start.

There are too many naysayers to list here, too many people who wrote me off, said I'd never make it. They questioned my training, my ability and probably my sanity. There were sports doctors and physicians who said that what I was contemplating wasn't just stupid but also dangerous, and that the repercussions of trying would be severe.

But in this room are the true believers. Because even on the worst days, there was never a doubt we would get to Bondi. Even when we questioned the how of it all, no one thought, *Oh, we better stop.* It was only a question of revising our strategy, tinkering with our methodology.

And yet, even though we knew I'd get it done, disbelief still fills the air. I shouldn't have gotten to Bondi. I came undone early. I could barely lift my foot off the ground from day twelve. Every single step I took was doing damage, or so it seemed. But that's precisely what we're celebrating: our triumph over pain and those doubting voices. It was a journey so far from normality that it felt like transcendence. It demanded absolute commitment from everyone involved. These were seven weeks we'll never replicate in our lifetimes. Seven weeks that made us better people.

IT'S MIDNIGHT WHEN STAFF kick us out of the surf club. Outside, there's little to engage the senses besides the sound of breaking waves. Beneath the glare of streetlights we wearily make our way back to the main road and the QT Hotel, where James has booked us rooms for the night. There, we experience a level of luxury that feels strange, foreign. Brad passes out in the bath, still clutching his cheese platter, his resting face a picture of joy.

Jem and I can't sleep. The excitement of the last few hours is still coursing through our veins and there's no blend of herbal tea strong enough to calm us down. We talk about the last twenty-four hours, and the weeks prior. We talk about those nights when Jem awoke to me shiver-sweating through cling-wrap and heat gel, stuck in that nightmare in which I was running and yet falling further and further behind. There were moments when I wondered where it all might lead, if we'd emerge with our relationship intact. But I never wondered for long. Not a day passed when I didn't lean on Jemma or yearn to see her face at the twenty-kilometre rest stop. We did this together.

SUNLIGHT BASKS THE ROOM in a pearlescent glow. It's morning now and the ute is parked somewhere outside, needing to be moved if we're to avoid a parking fine.

Sadness arrives like a wave, first lapping at my feet, then suddenly pulling me under. I never gave a thought to what I'd do after the run. And now that I'm finished, I realise I don't have a goal.

For the past two years, every day has been about getting me to the finish line at Bondi. For the past seven weeks, every day has been imbued with a sense of meaning and purpose. But crossing the line has ripped that away. And now I can't help but think, *What now?*

How do you return to an existence in sepia when for seven weeks your world has been a technicoloured baptism by fire? How do you settle for the mundanity and minutiae of everyday life when you've experienced what it means to live life to its fullest?

I slip out of the hotel and find the ute. By eight in the morning, Bondi's streets have come to life. I spot a parking space and flick on my indicator. It's only when I start edging my way into the space that I see another car aiming for the same one.

I hold off, wondering if the other driver might acknowledge that I have first dibs. But instead, I'm abruptly cut off via the kind of reverse park you'd expect of a learner driver on speed.

When the car door opens, a woman emerges, a yoga mat tucked under her arm. And instead of thanking me for hanging back, she unleashes at me a slew of profanities that poisons the morning stillness. I can't help myself. A smile breaks out across my face as I dip my head out the window and offer a warm, 'Good morning!'

The real world is back. It hasn't waited for me to unpack the last seven weeks, to journal or philosophise. Instead, it's reared its grotesque head and stared me down. The day has just begun and already this woman thinks she's a victim – late to her yoga class, forced by some mulleted clown to reverse hurriedly into a car space that was rightfully hers all along. I don't know what I expected, but the speed of the reality check deflates me. If I thought the trials of the last seven weeks might have left an imprint on the collective consciousness, it's apparent I was delusional. I'm reminded that most people live in their own heads, which are largely impervious to external stimuli. If you want to change how you feel, how you act, how you respond to what's thrown at you, then change must come from within.

51

What happens when you achieve the thing to which you've dedicated the last two years of your life? What happens when the goal you pursued relentlessly is ticked off? What happens when the very thing that makes you the best version of yourself is done and dusted? How do you then find meaning in the monotony of daily life, when you're incapable of doing those things that gave you purpose? What then?

Days turn to weeks that turn to months, and still I grapple with these questions. Immediately after Bondi, it was like I was floating. High on excitement and satisfaction, I lived by day with a constant surplus of energy. And each night when my head hit the pillow, the relief I felt at not having to wake at an ungodly hour the next morning to don battered sneakers and hit the road was exquisite.

But a week on, the novelty has worn off, replaced by a gaping emptiness I have no clue how to fill.

Back home in Randwick, where Brad, Jemma and I share a place, we sink into a collective depression. We move slowly between rooms, occasionally exchanging knowing glances that say, in a nutshell, *What is our purpose now? Surely not this!*

Occasionally we venture out, but I'm not entirely comfortable with the attention I'm getting. And aside from the shrieks of fans, Sydney's constant noise is overwhelming. For seven weeks, we heard little besides the sound of rain on corrugated iron, the crunch of gravel, the drone of cicadas – and the road trains. City noise is something else entirely; a soundtrack of whirring coffee machines and social chat that buzzes around us like a swarm of locusts. It makes us feel anxious and unsettled. We feel, in a strange way, out of place, even out of our depth.

Mostly, we are lost. None of us had thought about life beyond the run. We left for Perth with the inkling we would return as changed people, but just how changed we feel has surprised us. The run done, our minds are vacant and searching, our eyes glazed with a desperate look that says, *What next?*

When I enter my garage gym, everything is just as I'd left it months ago. Affixed to a wall is a whiteboard on which I've scrawled:

No one died from busted knees. Comfort is for fucking pussies. Strength and purpose. Fight all the way to the fucking end.

Every morning before I left, I woke before my alarm sounded and came down here, where I stared at these words as if reading the most fundamental instructions for life. And in the evenings when I returned to this same space, coated in a dusting of concrete, I saw these words and knew that, for me, there could be no rest days – not when you're going after something like I was.

These are the words – powerful if vulgar – that allowed me to be better each day, to push through barriers. Now I look at them, try to draw strength from them, but my body has nothing left to give. I no longer have the eyes of a savage, a gaze locked and focused on its target. Everything is shutting down. My tank is empty.

A week. That's all it's taken for the comedown to happen, brutal as an angry ape. We soared, therefore we've plunged. I should have guessed it. You do something remarkable, something life-changing, but there's a kicker: nothing you do thereafter can match it.

That's how it feels. But maybe that's wrong. Maybe I just need to let mind and body rejuvenate, and then another grand plan will come to me, and I'll pursue it with every fibre of my being, no matter the cost.

52

One night, I find myself tormented by thoughts of the run. I wake in a cold sweat, my legs flailing beneath the sheets as though I'm out there again, shuffling in the darkness save for the low beam of my headtorch. Frightened, Jemma turns on her bedside light, then stares at my saliva dripping from the opposite wall. She shakes my shoulders, tries to jolt me awake. 'Nedd! You can't do that! You can't spit at the wall.'

Dazed, I turn to her, apologetically. I don't know what to say or how to describe the traumatic visions that play on loop as soon as my eyes close.

'Sorry, Jem,' I say. 'I thought I was running.'

Other times, I wake up screaming from dreams so vivid it takes me minutes to realise they are dreams. In them, I can feel the lashing winds as forbidding clouds hang low above the landscape. Water sprays up from bitumen as road trains hurtle past, too close for comfort. Then the collision comes and I'm reeling in a world of agony until my eyes open and I sit bolt upright to find I'm safe in my own bed.

I thought it would all be behind me now, that I could cross the trans-Australia run off my list and move on. But in these visions of the night, I'm trapped in some past moment in time – a moment when the pain was extreme, or a moment when I felt utterly defeated and broken.

If the dreams aren't enough to keep me in the past, then the lingering pain throughout my body does the job. Three days a week I go through an extensive recovery routine, moving from sauna to ice bath to cryotherapy chamber. Belly assures me that everything will be okay as he examines my muscles and tries to coax some life back into my hips and tendons, but the injury list is extensive: bone stress in my tibia; the worst case of tenosynovitis Belly's ever seen; Achilles tendon issues; patellofemoral pain; irritation and compression of my plantaris; IT band syndrome; an intrasubstance tear in my gluteus minimus; severe lower-back pain; loss of toenails; blisters; significant foot pain; attrition and irritation of the fat pads on my metatarsal heads; and bursitis in both feet.

The foot pain has proven as stubborn as any of my ailments. Even if you're not logging miles, you still use your feet to stand – and as soon as mine touch the floor each morning, it feels like I'm treading on broken glass. I start getting cortisone injections into the outside of both knees, along with injections of platelet-rich plasma in both hips – a procedure so excruciating I need to lean on Jemma as I hobble out after each session.

It's scary to think this is the body I now exist in, and that it will remain so for some time. Belly assures me I'll overcome these injuries, that before long I'll feel invincible again. And just as I did out there on the run, I trust his judgment completely.

I know I should grant myself a grace period, acknowledge that I've earned a rest. But any kind of inactivity goes against my nature. To sit idly is to watch as the days pass, and it terrifies me how easily this can happen.

Strangers approach me and express their disbelief at my run. For the most part their words are kind, but often there's a note of scepticism or a smart-alec tone.

One person asks me: 'If you were offered one million dollars for your homeless charity on the basis that you *don't* do the run, would you take the money?'

I don't hesitate. 'Absolutely not.'

In those ridiculous hypothetical circumstances, I'd find some alternative way to raise the money. But I was always going to run across Australia.

People see me waddling across the street, hips all but locked. Some appraise my battered figure at the tender age of twenty-three and feel an urge to protect me. But I don't want protection. The fact is my feats of endurance have served to focus my mind and clarify my principles. I know that I'm my best self when I'm nudging my limits, when I'm as tired as hell but still willing to go again, with a purpose behind my actions.

It's a sobering thought I might be shortening my life. From what I can gather, if I keep pushing myself the way I have been, I'll be lucky to make it to fifty-five. The pursuit of challenges that blow people's minds, that redefine what we think of as possible, is not a recipe for a long life. But here's the thing: I'm not interested in preserving my body for those twilight years. I'd prefer to live large in my prime than get to ninety and think, *Great, I'm still walking.*

At twenty-three, I know what it feels like to wring a day dry, to hit the mattress knowing you have nothing left to give. I also know the acceptable Plan B: to retire with a determination to try again tomorrow, to push harder and do better.

So many people get around assuming they're just going to keep on living, that there's plenty of time for everything. Hobbies are picked up and forgotten, passions get steamrolled by the need for security, tasks are deferred until tomorrow. Theirs is a mindset of, *I'll worry about that later*, or, *I'll do that when I'm rich*. They forget that nothing in life is guaranteed, including their own longevity.

In the grand scheme of things, so much of what we do and covet is insignificant. Money, cars, social status – it all amounts to nothing. But how we comport ourselves, how we interact with others, these things have the power to bring change that ripples on through generations.

We're too comfortable. We can order food via an app, communicate solely via a screen or laptop, secure transport to wherever with the touch of a button. We don't always realise it, but the effect of all this is deadening. Just as sickness gives meaning to health, death to life, discomfort gives meaning to pleasure. You can't truly experience the latter without knowing the former. Those who wonder whether I'd have blown off the run in favour of a massive, no-strings donation to We Are Mobilise miss the point entirely. The challenge is what invigorates me and gives me purpose. It's in the doing that I thrive.

For Matty and Belly, though, this stop-at-nothing mindset of mine is challenging. I don't understand the human healing mechanism and I never will. And while they know all about the musculoskeletal system and optimal training loads, they aren't equipped to deal with a mind so stubborn that it refuses to heed warnings sent from body to brain. All Matty can do is hold me back during training and deliver me to the starting line in the best shape possible. All Belly can do is treat and protect me as the injuries arise. Both know it's inevitable that I'm going to bury myself again, go further than I've ever done before.

TWO MONTHS AFTER ARRIVING at Bondi and I wake up still unable to do the thing – run – that brings me the sharpest sense of purpose. I'm cranky and frustrated at my body's failings. In doing the thing I set out to do, I've also gone and wrecked myself.

I want to get up and attack the day, but my energy is still low, and my body is still pleading for rest.

I don't need to tell Belly, though, that as soon as I feel a stirring in my chest, I'll be out there again. I won't be waiting for a full recovery before I go out and run, say, sixty kilometres, or 100. Belly understands that this is who I am and what I do. And I won't settle for anything less.

53

If all good things take time, great things happen all at once. Change is here.

James is inundated with requests from TV stations and magazines wanting to interview me, while sponsorships are coming in thick and fast.

I'd left for Perth knowing I wouldn't be returning to my work as a tradie. But while I'm grateful for these new opportunities, I don't want my run to define me.

Internally, I'm hosting a conflict. It pits the part of me that wants to shun the spotlight and take on these challenges because that's what my mind and body desires, against the part of me that knows that, in broadcasting them to the world, I can inspire people while raising awareness on issues like homelessness. I don't know how to reconcile the two. I want eyes on the cause, not me. But it's through my attempts at doing what many deem impossible that the eyes turn.

It's been three months now and still I can't run – or do any sort of strength training. So, I spend my days doing the things I missed while out on the road. I take my Border Kelpie, Doug, to the dog park and watch as he runs free, kicking up dirt in the pursuit of birds who dare cross his path. I go to the beach in the eerie quiet of morning and immerse myself in the cold sea. I spend time with my family, with Jem and Brad – though a lot of the time we relive moments from the run.

Out and about, it seems like everyone feels they know me now. Is this what my new life will be like – people coming up to me in the supermarket, or calling out to me on the street? There's no way to hide anymore, no way back to my old life. Peace, as I knew it, is gone. And that might be okay if I can keep showing up and attacking the day.

People who approach me want to know what's next for me. And I don't blame them. I'd like to know that, too. But the more this question litters my social-media posts, the more it feels like external pressure, as opposed to the pressure I put on myself. It's one thing to chase goals of your own choosing; quite another to do stuff aimed at appeasing the masses.

I'm getting a little better at living in a quieter, more mundane present, in finding pleasure in the small things. I'm realising that not every moment of every day has to be distressing or intense to be worthwhile. Is that softness creeping in? Or is it maturity? I'm thinking the latter. I'm thinking that a life well lived is a life in which patience plays a role.

Patience isn't softness. I'm not retiring from the extremes, merely taking my time to choose the best method of re-entry. I don't know exactly what the future holds for me, but I do know there will be another challenge so great and alluring that it eats away at me, and I have no choice but to get out there and do it. I will find that challenge because I have no choice in the matter. I can't conceive of living my life without chasing the incredible every few years.

I feel the renegade spirit stirring within me, licking its lips at the thought of something rogue, unique, unheard of. I may have returned to normal life, but there's no shaking the memory of my run. My body moves differently now – slower, tighter. But it's far from done. Once you start testing the barriers you'd thought were indestructible, a whole new world opens up to you. Barriers are made to be broken. For me, soon, it will be time to smash some more.

EPILOGUE: TO THE MOON

We all need people who inspire us . . . But just as much as we need them, we need also to understand that we hold the answers ourselves.

Nedd

I'm at home in January 2023 when I get the call. They want me to deliver a keynote presentation in front of 3000 people at the Melbourne Convention and Exhibition Centre (MCEC). Then they add that I'll be opening for David Goggins.

'Would you be interested?'

'Fuck, yeah!'

I'd stumbled upon Goggins the way so many do – listening to a podcast on which he was telling his story. For the uninitiated, Goggins is a retired Navy SEAL who has been through Hell Week three times: five-and-a-half days of non-stop intense physical activity, including running, obstacle courses and paddling rubber boats in frigid waters. For those five days, trainees are put under significant mental and physical stress, all while facing brutal conditions in a severely sleep-deprived state. Not surprisingly, it's considered the toughest training in the US military, with only 25 per cent of SEAL candidates making it through.

Since then, he's completed more than seventy ultra-distance races and once held the world record for doing 4030 pull-ups in seventeen hours. The man is regarded as a demi-god by weekend warriors and professional endurance athletes alike. His resume is a seemingly endless list of achievements that point to an unbreakable mindset.

What attracts me to someone like Goggins isn't so much *what* he's done but *how*. For obvious reasons, I can't hear enough about a mentality that makes you push aside obstacles that would stop a stampeding rhino. Goggins is known for his 'Stay hard' mantra. He's a firm believer that to pull off great physical feats you don't have to be a born athlete, you just have to believe you can do them and refuse to quit until you have.

Despite my admiration for the guy, the thought of speaking in front of a few thousand people who've come to see a giant like Goggins has me on edge.

Assembling images from the finish at Bondi, I start crafting a presentation, without knowing exactly where it will lead. I write a speech and memorise it, matching word to images. There are some thirty slides in all.

A week out, I sit James down to be my practice audience. The run has made James and me close. I deeply appreciate the way he guides and protects me. We converse freely, telling each other home truths.

I stop speaking after thirty minutes, my allotted time. I look across the room at James, expecting to see him looking impressed. Maybe he'll even pull a Tom Cruise and jump up on the table, arms waving about as he lauds my newfound public-speaking prowess. But his expression is blank.

Oh shit, I think. *This is bad. Really bad.*

The silence seems to turn the air cold as I watch James shift uncomfortably in his seat. Then he looks at me.

'Mate, just tell your story,' he says. 'Just tell your story. What you've done and what was hard.'

I nod in faux understanding. But, clearly, I can't hide my confusion.

'Here, let's talk about it,' says James.

Together, we relive the run – its daily challenges and how we'd overcome them. It feels weird talking about those details with James, who knows them almost as well as I do. But in this interaction, I realise I've been going about the keynote all wrong. I've been too intent on delivering a speech that will help *everyone*. I want people of all ages and demographics to come away feeling inspired or having learned something. But in trying to relate to everyone, I'm in danger of resonating with no one. My speech is like a black-and-white drawing, screaming out for colour.

I understand then that I need to make this speech my own, much like I'd made the run my own. James helps me to see that my audience will join the dots between my story and theirs – that trying to do the joining for them won't work. They don't have to be runners or athletes, people attempting feats of endurance or hoping to run a marathon. Everyone has something that calls to their soul, that slices through layers of pragmatism and lands directly on the heart. These are the people I want to reach: the people who worry they've ignored that voice for too long and missed the chance to heed its summons.

Arriving in Melbourne, I decide to take a walk in the hope that fresh air and movement might relieve my nerves. I pace around the MCEC, marvelling at its size. A banner of Goggins stretches along the walls of the imposing structure. The keynote presents as a new kind challenge for me. That night, rehearsing alone in my hotel room, I tell myself I'm going to kill it.

I wake early and head out for an easy five-kilometre trot. My call time is 8:30 am. I move through the early-morning stillness and feel only excitement for the opportunity ahead. When I arrive at sound-check, I gaze at the tiered seating in disbelief. In a few hours this auditorium will be full.

Later, backstage, listening to the incessant buzz of the crowd, the enormity of the situation hits me, and my heart rate soars higher than it ever did on the run. The emcee introduces me:

'Today comes with a profanity warning. If you hate swearing, then my next guest is not the man for you, and nor is David Goggins.'

All I hear is my name and I step out from behind the tangle of curtains onto the stage and stand before a crowd that seems somehow surreal. I get just ten minutes into my speech when my mind goes blank. I freeze, feeling the weight of the audience that's now staring at me in shock. I clear my throat.

'Like I've always said, if you're going to shit the bed, you may as well do it in front of 3000 people.'

Laughter collides with my panic, blasting it into pieces. Suddenly, I feel comfortable again. *Look, everyone has come to see Goggins, not you. Relax. Share your story. And maybe inspire one or two people. Then fuck off home.*

And it all goes smoothly after that.

Sydney is the last stop on the Goggins tour and there I'm invited to an intimate dinner with the man himself – along with twenty others who've purchased the VIP package.

We meet at Rockpool Bar & Grill, an upmarket steakhouse in Hunter Street, Sydney. I'm used to the kind of eateries where there's no dress code, where footy shorts are fine. But this space screams opulence and I'm feeling a little out of place.

A long table is set up with ten seats on either side and one at the head. We all sit down, not knowing what to expect. Then someone official issues a series of instructions.

'Okay, a few rules, ladies and gents. Don't ask David for a video saying "Fucking fire up" to send to your mates. Second, there will be time for every single person here to tell him your story and ask him a question. We'll go around the table, but please, be good people. Be respectful and understand he's a person, too. Just know that everyone will have time.'

We all nod in agreement and, before we can return to our conversations, Goggins walks in. Guests start shifting their seats, trying to get a better view, while the whole table seems to come alive with a palpable energy.

There's a magnetism radiating out of Goggins. Other than a handshake, I haven't received any acknowledgement from him. But I feel it there in his presence; there's an energy, something I feel connected to.

Over food and wine, guests share their personal accounts of what it was that led them here to Goggins. They tell him what an inspiration he's been and why he's the reason they've run marathons or ultra-endurance events, got into fitness in their forties, found success in whatever field.

People ask him for help in finding themselves, or the partner of their dreams, or their best career path. Goggins mostly listens and nods and gives thanks.

At one point, a father asks him how he can protect his kids and ensure they don't have to endure the financial struggles and hardships he faced growing up. Goggins is silent for a few moments, then says, 'It's the struggle that made you.

So many parents have had to work so hard for their money that they don't want their kids to struggle like they did. But that's what made you so powerful and now you want to stop your kid from earning anything because it was hard? *Of course it's going to be hard.* You have to work for it.'

His finger shoots up, pointing across the table at me. 'This motherfucker had to work for it. One hundred kilometres a day! One hundred kilometres a day?'

I nod.

'For how many days,' he asks, turning to me now.

'Forty-six.'

'Forty-six motherfucking days. And how much sleep did you get a night? Three hours?'

'Yeah, sometimes three. Sometimes less.'

'Less than three hours.' He pauses, unspeaking, and turns back to address the rest of the table.

'He fucking showed up. That's how you do it. You've got to work for it. Your kids are going to watch you work for it. Don't talk the talk, do it.'

When it's my turn to share my story, I fix my eyes on Goggins. I see him not as an idol to be revered, but as an equal. In the past, I had used his story and messages as inspiration when I needed to, but I'd also known when to shut him off. I'd watched his videos and absorbed his 'stay hard' mantra, and then I had cultivated that attitude alone, becoming my own source of motivation. I had read his long list of achievements and thought, *Why can't I do something similar*? And then I'd gone out and achieved things for myself.

'David, I have an insatiable hunger for pain,' I tell him. 'I hate running, just like you, but I do it for what I get out of it. I know that when I do run, it brings something more than just fitness; it's a tool for life. I found you in 2019, but when I looked at you, I thought, *That's cool. What's his mindset to enable him to do what he does*? And then I went, *Okay, I'm going to do this my own way*. I don't want to say, "Stay hard". I want to say, "Keep showing up" and "To the fucking moon". I want to be me. I want to be authentic to myself and I want to do this my own way. And the fact I can sit here and tell you that means you've done your job.'

A silence falls over the table. Knives and forks have been put down. My fellow guests look uneasy, perhaps because what I'd said was a radical departure from the tales of adoration and hero-worship that they'd been telling.

Unfazed, I keep going.

'The way you watered down what you went through – I know you did. In your book, you talk about your bone injury and the pain you went through, but you don't talk about that fucking place that you have to go to get through it. I get that, because every single keynote I do, I can't tell people because it will go so far over their heads.'

Goggins looks at me and my whole body tenses. There's a connection between us – and he feels it, too.

'There's an energy here, brother,' he says, nodding his head.

A hand shoots up from the back of the table.

'Why can't you tell us? Why can't you tell us what you've been through, what the feeling is?'

I look at the bloke. 'Do you want me to answer, or Goggins?'

He points at me.

'If I was a heart surgeon and you came up and said, "Righto, I'm going to do this open-heart surgery", you'd have no idea what to do and I wouldn't be able to explain it to you because you haven't done years and years and years of it,' I say. 'In the same way, I've put myself in this scenario time and time again, so that now if I talk to someone who's done it too, they understand.'

Goggins interjects. 'And you'd think we are complete fucking masochists if you heard what we had to go through. You'd think we were deadset psychopaths, because to go to that place is not what the average person does. They throw in the towel when it gets hard.'

In the cab home that night, I feel closer to unlocking the answers to those questions of legacy that have been plaguing me for months. People will try to be someone else to impress the people they admire. They'll contort themselves to fit a new identity or persona, but it doesn't take long before the mask begins to slip and when it does, the idea of confronting reality is too daunting. We all need people who inspire us, who share their stories and battle scars, who show us almost anything can be achieved if you want it badly enough. But just as much as we need them, we need also to understand that we hold the answers ourselves, and that if we turn inwards, it's there we'll find the tools to unlock all manner of possibilities.

IN 2019, REIGNING UFC middleweight champion Israel 'The Last Stylebender' Adesanya came up against Kelvin Gastelum in the Octagon. Having won rounds one and four on all the judges' scorecards, Gastelum clearly wasn't going to make it easy for Adesanya.

Both fighters were physically spent, bodies glistening with sweat, faces bloodied and thick from pummelling. But still the eyes were large and determined. You knew instantly that both wanted the title and would do anything to get it. But where Gastelum was trying his best to project confidence, Adesanya didn't need to. He'd already seen the fight play out countless times behind his eyes. He'd seen himself deliver blow after blow, his feet still light, dancing in the ring. His every punch calculated, his legs poised to strike, his breath calm and controlled.

So, when the fourth round was called and Gastelum sunk into his stool, struggling to take in enough oxygen, Adesanya remained standing. He looked at his opponent and said, 'You can't beat me, I am prepared to die.' Gastelum could only nod his head.

When the fight resumed, the champ dropped Gastelum three times. The title was, as Adesanya had always known it would be, his.

When I watched this fight, I saw in Adesanya someone driven by a mindset similar to my own. And driven he is, not only to succeed, but to test his limits. His mentality is less, 'Win-at-all-costs' than, 'My capabilities are limitless'.

Adesanya knows that once you make a decision, you commit to it. For that reason, a poster of Adesanya hung in my garage gym in the lead-up to my cross-country run. Every day, I looked at that poster and knew a time would come when Adesanya and I would meet. As with Goggins, I feel a kinship with Adesanya, a brotherhood based on a shared energy, a shared determination to obtain what we seek.

Sure enough, Adesanya had got wind of my run and sent both words of encouragement and a donation to the cause. Receiving his support made me feel buoyant, like I could rise to any challenge. When Adesanya tells you something, you're not getting empty platitudes or lines from Hollywood movies; you're getting the hard-won wisdom of someone who's been in pitch-black places and lived to tell the tale.

By chance, Fox Sports approaches me. They want me to interview Adesanya in person in New Zealand before his title fight against Alex Pereira at UFC 287 in Miami in April 2023.

'Absolutely,' I say.

My passport expired in 2018 and the new one arrives a matter of days before my flight to Auckland. A camera crew follows me as I make my way to City Kickboxing, where Adesanya trains. Their presence annoys me; what should be a pure and private experience is being infiltrated by outside forces.

But as soon as Adesanya appears, I forget about the cameras. I note his two diamond earrings and the smile he directs my way. 'You motherfucker,' I call out with a laugh.

We embrace without awkwardness; there's a sense of old mates meeting up after a break. He looks me up and down: 'You're way taller than I thought.'

I watch him train with the relentless focus of an animal on the hunt. Later, in an ice bath, we talk about everything – our families, our aspirations, what we want to achieve before we leave this planet.

When we hop into a lift after spending the day together, I tell him, 'This was always meant to happen for me. I know you don't know this now, but at some point, I hope you will.'

I expect him to be put off by my frankness, but he just turns to his brother and flashes a grin. 'We'd love you to be there [the fight]. Can you get to the States?'

Yes, I can. I fly out for UFC 287.

When I step off the plane in Miami, I feel numb, rudderless and lost in a sea of people, many of them seemingly hostile, as if this bloke with a mullet has gotten in their way. It's the first time I've travelled overseas alone and I'm still a bit down on energy. Here, I feel I've been thrust into an environment where everything is in overdrive.

A taxi takes me from Miami International Airport to the Kaseya Center, the venue for the fight. Inside, fans fill the stadium all the way up to the nosebleed sections, where it still feels as though you're directly above the action and able to feel the impact of each strike.

Long before Adesanya and Pereira walk out for the main event, the atmosphere is electric. There's a stench of booze and body odour as the hours tick by and voices become hoarse. Donald Trump makes an appearance. Music blasts through the speakers. Finally, the gladiators emerge to a tidal wave of sound that could shatter bone.

The fight starts explosively. Adesanya looks frighteningly intense. It's evident to everyone how switched on he is; he's reading Pereira's attacks like they're idiot boards, then countering.

It's a waiting game, each of the fighters playing cat and mouse. Pereira's kicks start to take a toll on Adesanya's legs, but it's too late. Adesanya catches Pereira, delivering three strikes in quick succession, and finishing with a hammerfist on the ground. It's all over. The crowd erupts. In my euphoric state, I watch as two guys pass out from screaming.

By some stroke of luck, I find myself out the back where all the fighters and celebrities are hanging out, speaking to reporters. I see Adesanya talking to the UFC panel, beaming with pride. I hang back, conscious that this is his moment and not wanting to bother him, his entourage or the close friends who press forward to congratulate the champ.

But then Adesanya spots me, points and calls my name. 'Nedd! Nedd! Come here.'

He hugs me, then pulls back and we lock eyes.

'The power of the human mind,' he says. 'The power of the human spirit. It was right there.'

THE NIGHT PASSES IN a blur at E11EVEN nightclub. When I finally extract myself from the after party, the sun's already up and I'm still running on the fumes of jet-lag and adrenaline, feeling unmoored in this great expanse that is Miami. I know the hangover is going to be bad tomorrow, but how often does one get to have a night like this?

Unable to sleep, I rise at 4 am to run as UFC revellers continue to spill out of nightclubs. Striding out along Miami Beach, I see movement coming from under the MacArthur Causeway Bridge. Voices carry upwards and I see figures clustered around one another, seeking warmth and refuge. Just hours ago, I was in a club surrounded by people spending exorbitant sums in search of a buzz. Now, I look out and see some fifty forlorn souls living on makeshift beds, looking for all the world as though they might be discarded along with the rubbish piles that have built up around them.

When dawn breaks and cafes begin opening their doors, I start making my way back to the hotel.

'Hey yo!' comes a friendly greeting.

I turn to the guy calling me and gesture towards the nearest cafe.

'Can of Coke, chips, burger,' comes his order.

'Anything else?' I say, smiling.

'That's it. Thanks, man!'

When the food is ready, I walk back to him and watch him take the meal with eyes full of gratitude. But as I survey the horde of people living under the bridge, I feel a kind of paralysis. Where does one begin? How does one start to help? It leaves me rattled. Adequate housing should be a right afforded to everyone, but according to the Department of Housing and Urban Development, some 582,000 Americans experienced homelessness in 2022, a number that's most likely a gross underestimate.

In Adesanya, I see someone capable of manifesting success. It's like he's writing his own story in advance, certain of how each chapter will end. He knows if he sets his mind to something and works towards it, it will happen because no one can take away his work ethic, no one can stop him fighting until the end. It was something I channelled during the run, but now it is something I know I will channel for my cause.

Since I ran across Australia, people continue to ask me: 'Now that you've raised money for homelessness, what's the next charity going to be?'

They don't understand that raising a block of money is not enough. The issue of homelessness is too great, too complex to be wiped out by a single donation, however large. Homelessness is not a flavour-of-the-month plaything for virtue signallers. It is a global crisis and, like Adesanya, I can see the difference that I have the power to make. For me, there's no stopping until I make it.

I THOUGHT IT HAD been just Australians getting behind the run, but when legendary American outdoorsman Cameron Hanes contacts me, I realise the message of showing up knows no borders.

The man is an absolute predator, someone for whom the need to test his limits is baked into his DNA. There are no days off for this guy. On any given day, Hanes is out in the wilderness with his bow, or strength training, or running up a mountain somewhere. He does what he does to satisfy a desire that burns within.

So, when he asks me if I want to meet up with him in Oregon to shoot bows, run and record a podcast, I happily accept. I know that whatever Hanes chooses to put me through will be tough – and that's good. Bring it on. In my recovery, I'm now up to running ten kilometres at a time, though still feeling my knees crunch and hips protest with every stride. Sans adrenaline, I feel every niggle. I'm wondering if I'll get back to how I was or if the damage I've done to myself is for good, a memento of the journey. Whatever the case, I can't say no to this opportunity.

I'm flying from Boston to Oregon. Cam and I are scheduled to run the next morning at the civilised hour of 8 am, but when my flight lands at 10:30 pm, I tell him I'll be starting early – at midnight. No matter the terrain, I just want to start, I say. I can always meet up with him somewhere along the way. But Cam has other ideas. 'Let's make some epic-ness,' he says.

I've barely slept, but when midnight rolls around, I'm buzzing from an energy that comes with knowing suffering awaits. There's a sense of fear of the unknown; not knowing when your body will crumble, or when your mind will begin bargaining with you to stop as you try desperately to cut through the noise and stay in the fight. I relish the feeling. With my running pack on, its compartments loaded with sachets of energy gel, I feel like my old self. *This is Nedd*, I think. *This is what I do.* As I step out into the frosty morning air, Cam pulls up in his truck.

It's time to go. Let's do this.

Lane County Oregon is cold in April and as we run stride for stride, elbows jostling as we search for a shared rhythm, our breath fans out before our faces, momentarily blocking our vision. Out on the trails, I say to Cam, 'We've got 100 kilometres ahead – we're doing 100 kilometres.'

With his good-natured humour and competitive spirit locked in, Cam laughs. I don't know anyone who's had 100 kilometres sprung on them and not baulked, but I want him to know I'm up for the challenge and he matches my desire to test myself.

When we hit the fifty-kilometre mark, I can't help but smile. 'Halfway, Cam.'

He takes me off trail and there, looming before us, is Mount Pisgah, an imposing, near-vertical hill that rises some 320 metres above the surrounding Willamette Valley. Cam gestures to a rock and tells me about today's challenge. The first time Cam hoisted this thirty-two-kilogram rock on his shoulder and walked up Mount Pisgah, it took him two hours. Now, his fastest time is 36 minutes 30 seconds. According to Cam, the fastest time any podcast guest has achieved is forty-nine minutes.

'Easy. Let's do it,' I say.

As if wanting to protect me from my own delusions, Cam adds, 'There's only been one person who ever got it done on this podcast, and he just *had* to get it done. But no one else has actually finished it on their own.'

But his words land too late. I've already wrapped my hands around the cool surface of the rock and started bringing it up towards my shoulder.

It's heavy, there's no denying that. My whole body goes rigid underneath it, my core straining to keep me upright. I can feel it digging through my shirt into my flesh. Every few metres, I need to adjust its position, shuffling it from shoulder to shoulder.

Shocked by the steepness of the ascent, my whole body's screaming. I feel my quads cramping, my calves quivering and threatening to tear. But I know I have to get to the top. I want to stand there knowing I've overcome the cautiousness that has filtered into my body since the run, holding me back.

When we finally reach the top, I look down at my watch.

'Thirty-eight minutes and thirty seconds,' I tell Cam.

We run sixty kilometres all up, following up the miles with some bow shooting and lifting, then diving deep into a conversation about life, goals and the pursuit of pain.

When I get back to my hotel that night, I feel invigorated. A familiar comfort spreads over me: heavy legs, joints aching; the unhelpful thoughts that had been bouncing around in my head have been silenced, leaving nothing besides the satisfaction of exhaustion.

I know from this moment that there will be no more cautiousness, no more days of switching off the GPS at the ten-kilometre mark simply because it's the safer option, a directive in a rehabilitation program prescribed by sports doctors.

I'm back, baby, inhabiting the mindset I thrive in: a contempt for bodily pleas to stop.

I am zeroing in on my next challenge. Thoughts and ideas have come to mind at various times since finishing the run, but none of them has imbued in me the all-encompassing desire that running across Australia had.

Now, I have it! A run that will prove even more mentally and physically testing than traversing Australia. Whether he knew it or not, the day's efforts with Cam had made up my mind.

I'm back. And I'm good to go.

THE ALARM SOUNDS AT 3:30 am and in the darkness I fumble for my shorts and runners. Winter has arrived overnight. There is no easing into it, just suddenly frosted windows and fridge-like air. The streets are empty as the kilometres rack up.

The sun rises, casting Centennial Park in a soft light. I see fat dew drops on grass, trees devoid of leaves, odd knick-knacks discarded on the ground, a jumper left dangling on a fence post. My pace is quick, my breathing easy. There is no straining, no grimacing, just a look, I suspect, of serene composure born of an appreciation for movement, freedom and a beating heart.

It's still dark when I get home, but there's action on the streets now. A jogger appears, shuffling awkwardly on the street corner, waiting for his watch to start, unwilling to take a step until everything is being tracked and timed.

I head to the South Coogee stairs and grab hold of a rock, the biggest one I can find. Since climbing Mount Pisgah with Cam, ascending under load has become a staple of my training, making for the best full-body workout I've ever done in under an hour. I set the timer for sixty minutes and hoist the rock onto my shoulder. Instantly, I feel my quads tense, and with the stairs in front of me, I begin, climbing up and down, up and down, for what seems like an eternity.

Since my run across Australia, life for me has changed. There's no standard week for me anymore. I quit working as a tradie and have instead been driven to share my story and see it connect with others. Constantly, I find myself asking: *Why me?* I still don't have the answer, but I do know that to have a platform and to be given opportunities to inspire is a privilege. And with privilege comes responsibility. Change can be hard, but it comes regardless of whether we're ready or not, and I can only welcome the possibilities my run has created for me.

Some have asked if I might hang up the running shoes and take it easy. After all, they say, you've earned that right.

But I'm twenty-four years old and cannot view my run across Australia as anything other than one chapter in the story of my still-young life. What I learned from that experience is that there is no return to normality. When you've tasted what it is to dance on the edge, walking the well-trodden path is no longer an option. Colour seems to dim, sounds no longer carry clarity, and those things people hold as priorities – wealth, security, stability – to me they are mere distractions, empty and meaningless. And try all you like to fit in, when you're wired like me, you never will. Once you've heeded that maverick voice, it never stops calling you, a little louder and more insistent each time.

In two years' time, I won't be talking about my run across Australia anymore. By then I'll have completed this new challenge (the details of which I'm not quite ready to disclose), the very thought of which is setting me alight.

Try to break records by all means, knowing that in going for them you might come up short. But the truth is, records are secondary to the doing. Life is about showing up and going hard, not for recognition or reward but because the striving and the discipline – and, yes, the suffering – make you a better person. When an enticing opportunity presents itself, don't hesitate. There is never a right time to start, so dive in. You take something away from every experience. Even if you don't win, you learn.

I don't often voice my goals to people because doing so can be counterproductive. Most people are more comfortable expressing their doubts than they are getting behind you; they want to tell you why your mission can't be done, that you're dreaming, that you're naïve or childish.

But I'll tell you now: in ten years' time, I will have gotten 10,000 people off Australia's streets. Like any physical challenge, I know it will take an immense amount of work and a team of committed people to pull this off. But I also know that it can be done.

Seven months have passed since the run when I get a text from Noah at We Are Mobilise.

Nedd, just wanted to let you know the first person from our employment pathway has officially secured a job, starts full-time in construction on Monday. Funds from your run will go directly to those in this pilot, paired with job and housing support. The first of many, my brother, many lives are going to be changed.

Tears moisten my cheeks as I reread the message again and again, the words finally sinking in. To see change occur is incredible. It's the reason I do what I do. I think of my parents, who taught me the value of giving back. If the run had been all about me, it would still have been remarkable and unforgettable but not *important*. To tie your dreams to a purpose: that's how to give your life meaning.

To make a mark on this world you don't need to be born with any great gifts, athletic or otherwise. You just need the imagination to picture something amazing and then the audacity to start going after it. And whatever you do, you need to make it your own; you need to turn off the noise and even the monologues from your heroes and listen to your own voice calling to you until you go, 'Oh, my God, I won't waste another day until I get this done.' And when you believe it, anything is possible.

To the moon.

ACKNOWLEDGEMENTS

SHOWING UP, like all good books, was a team effort. When Simon & Schuster said they'd like to be my publisher, my first instinct was 'shit yeah, that's mad', and then it very quickly turned to 'I just scraped through Year 12 English, so how on earth do I write a book?' How do I cram all my thoughts and emotions over the previous eight months and beyond into a book while making the words resonate to sound more like me than I do myself? I was introduced to Jess Campbell in June 2022 when she wrote a piece about me in a magazine promoting my cross-country run. We instantly clicked over a Zoom chat and spent the best part of an hour talking about who I am, where I've been, what I've done and what I'm going to do. I left that Zoom excited for what was about to be written but I'd had plenty of articles written before so I started to think it couldn't be that good. Could it? COULD IT??? What Jess wrote after only speaking with her for an hour was truly remarkable. When seeking out who I'd get to help write my book there was only ever going to be one person. I want to thank Jess for the countless hours spent learning everything about me while we chomped down on some biltong and laughed for hours on end. I'm proud of you, Jess, the incredible writer that you are, but most importantly the incredible person you are. Thank you, Jess.

To the Bursty Company, more specifically James Ward (Jimmy) and Adrian Goold. These guys had left their jobs to start Bursty, a marketing agency that was born to create, collaborate and tell stories that matter, after feeling disillusioned in a job they felt was no longer fulfilling. Post 50-in-50, I was given Jimmy's number through a family friend. I didn't even know why we were talking the day we made contact, but I knew something good was going to come of it. I think the universe brought us together for a reason much greater than either Jimmy or I know at this point in time. There are very few people like Jimmy. He is a combination of empathy and compassion and is devoted to those he considers his people. He gets boundlessly excited around ideas he knows will contribute to his strong desire to do good in this world and he is a genuinely good man. Both James and Adrian have taught me a lot of valuable lessons over the past three years and there's a certain energy around when we all get together. Thanks, James, for trusting that I am a man of my word. It took a lot of guts to believe in a very inexperienced twenty-one-year-old and to show the level of support you, Adrian and your team did. You took a risk and I know the rewards will continue to come. Special thanks to Richie Butterworth, Sam Dennis, Sam Starkins, Gill McPhee, Lincoln Cottee, Will Carter, Jay Rowlings, Ryan Earles, Emily Maciver, Xavier Cordier, Jesse Toniolo and Justin Lee who worked tirelessly behind the scenes at Bursty to help bring the run together.

To the weapon that is Hannah Watkins. From the day you reached out to me at the coffee shop during my 50-in-50, you have been an integral part of my story. Your support, that in the beginning was purely for the love of being involved, has been unwavering. I am grateful each day that you are in my corner and that I get to work alongside someone that I now consider a dear friend. Thank you, Hannah, for believing in me also.

To Noah Yang and the whole team at We Are Mobilise. Who would have thought! Noah, your zest for life and desire to help people less fortunate is something we should all try to emulate. The world would be a much better place if everyone spent a day with you. Thank you for all the work you do with our friends on the street. My dream is that we can continue to make a powerful impact that will put an end to homelessness. This is just the beginning, my friend.

To Hamish Blake. It should feel weird even writing that name for an acknowledgement in this book, let alone having him write the foreword, but it doesn't. It feels perfectly correct. Hame and I found a common ground through his rock-solid support and constant entertainment on my run from the very beginning. It took the form of a donation and then many written, voice and video messages, always bringing a laugh when I needed it most. When I finally met Hame in the flesh at Bondi, it felt like I'd known him my whole life. I can't honestly imagine him not being in it now. Aside from the quick-witted humour and his ability to bring light to any situation, I think his greatest attribute is that he treats everyone equally. Thanks, Hame, for being you, and for being my mate.

To Sam Dennis, the boy from Torquay. The man with the cinematic vision. Thank you for embracing the craziness of a group of people you had literally never met before to immerse yourself inside a bubble that, at times, felt both impenetrable and unhinged. Thank you for being a team player, for your compassion and your respectful withdrawal when it was needed. You made a mark on all of us while you were able to capture the rawness of our experience and the mind-blowing landscape of this great country. I am extremely grateful for you. Also, who would have thought we could have turned a vego into a meat-eater in just 46½ days!

To my on-road team, Mum, Dad, Jem, Brad, Belly and Sam: I can't believe we made it out alive with unbeatable memories and unbreakable bonds.

To Tom Hunt, I am grateful to have met you. To many more memories.

Now of course this whole journey wouldn't be quite the same without the following incredible people and businesses, so I want to thank and acknowledge the role they have all played in helping me but also helping my mission and purpose.

To Pancho Gutstein, Neysa Goh, Britt Austin and the PUMA team – thank you for believing in me. It takes a special group of people and a brand that's willing to take chances to trust a wet-behind-the-ears twenty-one-year-old to run across the country. From being my main run partner to my now proud partner: all the amazing people at Case Construction, McIntosh and Sons and EEA, especially Chris Newton and Paul Davies for getting the partnership off the ground. Adam Linforth, Jess West, Jimmy Exelby and Brendan Hartman and all the legends at Budgy Smuggler – you were the first! More schnitty meetings soon. Trent and Brooke Cotchin from Posisocks, looking forward to working with you both.

Thanks to all the amazing people and organisations at Pilot Health, BCF, Blue Dinosaur, Let's Go Motor Homes, St Food Co, Jetstar, ReMilk, Boss Hunting, Optimum Nutrition, Running Heroes, Westpac, Swell Coffee, Merton Lawyers, MRDG, the mighty Forbes Rugby Club, Skip the Dealer, Team Global Express, North Bondi RSL, Better Beer, the Melbourne Rebels, BRC, the Parramatta Eels and the Parramatta Leagues Club, Hyped Media, Swinging Bridge Estate, the Meta Team, Curly Lewis Beer, North Bondi Surf Lifesaving Club, the NSW Government and Premier Dominic Perrottet, Cisco, Jellis Craig and Isagenix for either sponsoring the run or making significant donations to Mobilise.

Thanks also to Matty Abel, Michael Rugendyke, Amy Quinnell, Mark Gade, James Want, Jack Slade, Jack Steele, Matt Ford, Kirsty Wilson, Russell Conway, Gregg Porteous, James Henry, Jason Nicholas, Alex Fraser, Pat Cunningham, Paul Docherty, David Rennex, Tim Smith, Scott Cam, Mark Bouris and Matty J. And special thanks to Jo, Edie and Darcy for looking after Doug, the hardest job of all!

Thanks to Jimmy Barnes for your unwavering support but most of all for bringing my rock and roll dreams to life. Singing on stage with you at Cockatoo Island will be a memory I cherish forever.

Thanks to the team at Simon & Schuster for making this book a reality.

To the people on the road from Cottesloe to Bondi – the truckies, the roadhouse owners, the accommodation suppliers, the supporters, the police – every one of you played a role in the story of my run – thank you.

To the people of Bedgerabong, Forbes and the Kinross community – thanks for all your support across the years.

And finally, to the 37,000 plus people who donated: you are the reason we can make such a big impact on homelessness in Australia. This is just the start.

ABOUT THE AUTHOR

Nedd Brockmann grew up on his family's farm in Central West New South Wales before moving to Sydney to work as a sparky in 2019. At the age of twenty-three, he became the fastest Australian to run across the country, and the second-fastest in the world, completing a journey of 3953 kilometres from Perth's Cottesloe Beach to Sydney's Bondi Beach in 46 days and 12 hours.

Averaging an incredible 85 kilometres a day for the run, Nedd had to contend with numerous challenges along the way, from the logistical nightmares of accommodation and food supplies out in the Australian Outback, to countless injuries that threatened to derail him from finishing. With a determination to succeed and an aptitude for endurance, Nedd continued to show up each day with the resolution he would finish, and in doing so inspired thousands.

Throughout the run, he used his platform to call attention to the urgent crisis of homelessness, setting himself the target of raising a million dollars for the charity We Are Mobilise, who provide functional care to the homeless and seek to create change through connection. In his regular posts on Instagram, Nedd highlighted the highs and lows of the epic run and encouraged others to pursue their dreams; to trust in their ability to overcome adversity and have the courage to start on those lofty goals that otherwise might prove daunting. It's no surprise that when he made his way to Bondi Beach, a crowd of more than 10,000 people gathered to welcome him home, all of them feeling a kinship to his laid-back humour and authentic self. It was a finish that is now woven into the national fabric of Australian history.

With support coming from truckies on the road, farmers, kids doing bake stalls, families, sportsmen and running enthusiasts alike, Nedd raised a final total of $2.6 million for We Are Mobilise, with $600,000 raised on the final day of the run. It's a figure that has already seen change occur in real time, with We Are Mobilise providing an Australia-first direct cash transfer program for the homeless aimed at offering employment and ongoing support, including housing and financial counselling. Just eight months after completing his run across Australia, We Are Mobilise reported their first participant had received a contract offer to start work.

Though Nedd doesn't call himself a runner or athlete, he is someone who sees tests of physical endurance and stamina as a playground for the human spirit to thrive. He takes on such challenges with nothing but a desire to test himself and prove that anything is possible if you're willing to work hard for it and pay the price.